MORE THAN PETTICOATS

Remarkable Indiana Women

Rachel J. Lapp
Anita K. Stalter

TWODOT®

GUILFORD, CONNECTICUT
HELENA, MONTANA
AN IMPRINT OF THE GLOBE PEQUOT PRESS

A · TWODOT® · BOOK

Text design by Nancy Freeborn
Map by M. A. Dubé © Morris Book Publishing, LLC

Library of Congress Cataloging-in-Publication Data
Lapp, Rachel J.
  More than petticoats. Remarkable Indiana Women/Rachel J. Lapp, Anita K. Stalter.—1st ed.
      p. cm.—(More than petticoats series)
  Includes bibliographical references.
  ISBN-13: 978-0-7627-3806-9
  ISBN-10: 0-7627-3806-5
  1. Women—Indiana—Biography. 2. Women—Indiana—History. 3. Indiana—Biography. I. Stalter, Anita K. II. Title. III. Title: Remarkable Indiana Women.

CT3262.I5L36 2006
920.72'09772—dc22

                                                        2006019951

Manufactured in the United States of America
First Edition/First Printing

DEDICATION

To Marcella Rocke Stalter, a remarkable woman in our lives, and in memory of Esther Good Lapp.

CONTENTS

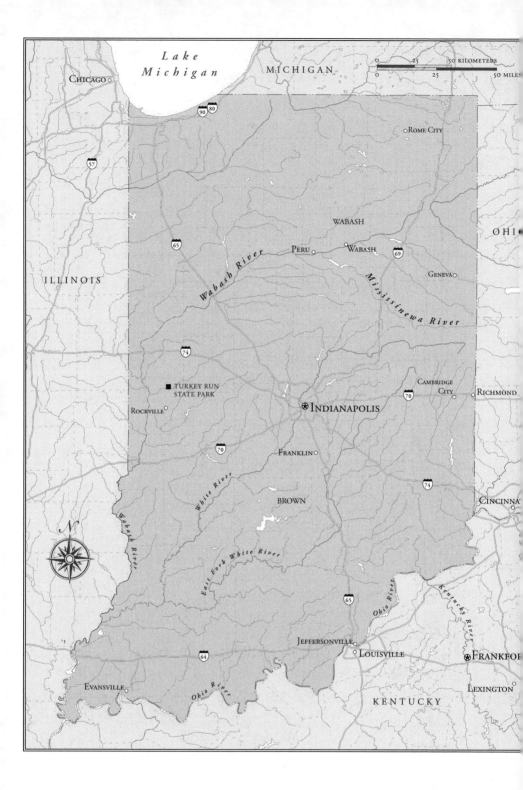

Lake Michigan

MICHIGAN

CHICAGO

ILLINOIS

○ROME CITY

WABASH

PERU○ ○WABASH

GENEVA○

Wabash River

Mississinewa River

OHI○

■ TURKEY RUN
STATE PARK

ROCKVILLE○

⊛ INDIANAPOLIS

CAMBRIDGE
CITY

○ RICHMOND

FRANKLIN○

White River

BROWN

CINCINNA

Wabash River

East Fork White River

Ohio River

Kentucky River

JEFFERSONVILLE○

○ LOUISVILLE

⊛ FRANKFO

EVANSVILLE○

Ohio River

KENTUCKY

LEXINGTON○

25 KILOMETERS · 50 KILOMETERS

25 · 50 MILES

INDIANA

INTRODUCTION

"I could not, at any age, be content to take my place by the fireside and simply look on. Life was meant to be lived. Curiosity must be kept alive. One must never, for whatever reason, turn his back on life."

—Eleanor Roosevelt

"Because of their age-long training in human relations—for that is what feminine intuition really is—women have a special contribution to make to any group enterprise."

—Margaret Mead

To open the brittle pages of a ledger filled with faded, handwritten records from the meetings of the Indianapolis Equal Suffrage Society is to open a revelation from the past. It is not unlike coming across an old journal of a mother or a grandmother and glimpsing, perhaps for the first time, a different season in her life—seeing her as a young woman wondering about her future, a new wife or mother noting the events of the day, or a household manager listing her purchases made or vegetables canned or visitors welcomed. This journal—with its broken spine and musty scent, filled with faint, spidery handwriting and yellowed newspaper clippings—reveals the passionate work of Indiana suffragists of more than a century ago. It shows how they joined other states and women's organizations in bringing about the societal transformations that led to the 1920 passage of the Nineteenth Amendment, which gave national voting rights to the country's female citizens. The liberties women take for granted today did not come about by natural evolution or chance.

In the early twenty-first century, the opportunities open to women are unparalleled—in education, in career development, in improving health and wellness, in finding creative outlets, in entering a broad spectrum of leadership positions. The barriers for understanding one another are far fewer today than ever before. Yet without learning about the lives of those women who once walked over the same ground as we do today, we lose a significant part of our collective history. And unfortunately, much of this history remains largely hidden, overlooked by most educational texts.

Indiana suffragists in the last decades of the nineteenth century identified this problem and made a commitment to right this wrong. They kept records of their own lives and work and began an initiative to convince various libraries to add materials on women's history and the suffrage movement to their collections. They also met with religious and educational leaders to share with them the goals and advances of the equal rights movement, seeking not to agitate but to build bridges. The suffragists at the turn of that new century were perhaps more radical in their ideas than those who came before, particularly when advocating for changing traditional roles and women's citizenship opportunities, but they appreciated their predecessors who had established and bequeathed to them the philosophical foundation for equal rights. All Hoosiers, men and women, benefit from the efforts of these generations of suffragists who wished for those to come to have a more inclusive understanding of the history of their state.

Today, in the twenty-first century, there are still those of us who remember to learn from the past, those who see that the progresses charted by our ancestors have made possible the lives we enjoy today. There are wonderful projects being initiated in many states to incorporate more fully the histories of women into public school curricula and the state museum collections. In Indiana, for example, two experienced teachers have worked to create a biographical database of Hoosier women to accompany instructional guides for elementary and middle school teachers.

As a mother-daughter team approaching this project, preparing to research and present the lives of pioneering women of Indiana, we realized that our first step would be to decide what our own roles would be in the authorship process. We had to consider our individual strengths and how they could best be used to present the stories of these women whose lives we had come to respect so deeply. By working together, we also felt we emulated the spirit of so many generations of women who have shared labor, ideas, and their lives.

There are biographical records of hundreds of Indiana women located in historical libraries and museums across the state. Many piqued our interest, from hardworking midwives of the early 1800s to organized suffragists of the early twentieth century, from farmers' wives laboring to sustain their families to urban schoolteachers promoting holistic education. When we began to narrow the list of potential subjects, we considered the eras in which they lived, their contributions to the state of Indiana (and beyond), the diversity in their backgrounds and life callings, and the spectrum of their cultural and religious experiences. We also had to consider the documents and narratives available to us so as to attempt to sketch as complete a portrait as possible. The lives of the women we eventually chose to include spanned 200 years and a broad range of interests and influences.

At first glance, a women's magazine columnist and a naturalist might not appear to have much in common, nor might an African-American entrepreneur and a queen of agriculture. But as we learned more about the lives of these women, we found a number of common strands. We saw that each life was shaped by the joys and responsibilities of family, education, and motherhood, as well as community obligations. Some were also moved to advocate for peace and justice in a world of inequities. We also found that the contributions of Indiana women have had a profound impact on the rest of the country, and even the world, in areas such as women's suffrage, environmental awareness, prison reform, teacher training and education, female entrepreneurship, humane housing standards, and much more.

The women profiled in this volume found a larger calling in their lives—personal, professional, educational, spiritual, societal— that often began close to home. Their work was usually inspired by a concern for others, starting with those immediately around them: their families, their neighbors, the classmates of their children, their pupils, their professional colleagues, the girls who reminded them of themselves. They found ways of using their skills to bring about profound change in their communities and state. These women were also supported by other women in their efforts, creating a sense of unity that often led to larger-scale movements.

We are indebted to the historians, journalists, authors, and artists who recognized the value of documenting the lives of Indiana women, as well as to those who left their own records—memoirs, newspaper interviews, books, photographs, and more—that reveal what they valued, how they viewed the world, and what they sought to accomplish. We wrote this book because we are eager to share and celebrate the stories of these women, and to, in some small way, weave together their lives with those of contemporary and future remarkable Indiana women.

—Rachel Lapp and Anita Stalter

FRANCES SLOCUM

1773-1847

Little Bear Woman

FRANCES SLOCUM HUDDLED ALONE AND SCARED UNDER THE stairway of her family's large farmhouse. She had just seen her mother snatch up the baby of the family and hurry outside, along with two of the other children, to take cover in some bushes. Five-year-old Frances had been told to hide indoors, but now she wanted the comfort of her mother's strong but surprisingly gentle hands. And what would happen to her father, who was out working in the fields?

A few moments earlier, a gunshot had sounded across the farmlands of Pennsylvania's Wyoming Valley. Though the Revolutionary War was still being fought between American colonists and British soldiers, Frances was experiencing an Indian raid, not a military battle. Indian attacks were common in the area near Wilkes-Barre where Quakers Jonathan and Ruth Slocum had settled to farm and raise their ten children.

Most of the 200-plus residents of the valley had already been killed or had abandoned their homes out of fear for their lives. But Jonathan Slocum wasn't afraid of the native Delaware people. Like his fellow Quaker, the illustrious leader William Penn (who had established good relations with Indian groups in Pennsylvania, and who, like Slocum, wore a black, broad-brimmed hat), Jonathan wanted to build trust with his native neighbors. But his eldest son, nineteen-year-old Giles, felt differently and had covertly joined with other settlers to fight the Indians.

The Delawares thought that the Slocums had turned against them and decided to strike. A group stormed the farm, and several Indians came into the house looking for food and useful items. They found little auburn-haired Frances instead, having seen her toes poking out beneath the stairs.

The raiders carried off Frances and her twelve-year-old brother Ebeneezer. Also taken was Wareham Kingsley, a neighbor boy who was in the Slocum's yard at the time. Seeing this, Ruth Slocum and one of her older daughters emerged from their hiding place to plead for their family members. Desperate, they pointed out that Ebeneezer's foot was crippled; the Delaware raiders could see this was true and let him go. The Slocums urged the Indians to release Frances as well, but could only watch as the barefoot child screamed for her mother as she was taken away. This was the last time Ruth would see her daughter, though she never gave up hope that Frances would return.

The day was November 2, 1778. It would be sixty years before Frances Slocum would see any member of her birth family again. She didn't know that Indians returned to the farm six weeks later and killed her father, Jonathan Slocum, and maternal grandfather, Isaac Tripp, also wounding her brother William. Remaining members of the family and their neighbors searched for Frances in the weeks and years to come but found no sign of her.

Six years after the kidnapping incident, as the American colonists continued to create an independent nation, Wareham Kingsley found his way back to the Wyoming Valley after being released from captivity. Unfortunately, he didn't know what had

FRANCES SLOCUM

happened to Frances because the two had been separated soon after their capture. Wareham provided some relief to the Slocums by telling them that Frances had been treated kindly: Her captors had given her food, carried her when she was tired, and given her moccasins to wear.

Ruth Slocum sent sons Giles and William to Niagara Falls in 1784, and then to Ohio in 1788. In both places, white people who had been taken as children by Indians were searching for their families. The Slocums didn't find Frances either time. How would they know her after so many years in a different culture, surrounded by an unfamiliar language and way of life? The brothers looked for a girl with a missing fingertip—Frances had been involved in a farm accident as a young child. The family offered a reward for information. Members of the Slocum family continued to travel to New York and Ohio to talk to children who had survived capture by Indians, but none had any information about Frances.

Twelve years after the kidnapping, Giles Slocum met a man named Colonel Thomas Proctor, who had been sent by the secretary of war early in 1791 to visit Native-American settlements around Lake Erie. Giles begged him to help his family by negotiating with the Indians who had taken Frances. A note in Proctor's travel journal dated a month later noted that he encountered Frances somewhere during his travels. However, he did nothing to inform the Slocum family.

Before Ruth Slocum died, twenty-eight years after the disappearance of Frances, she asked her children to continue to look for their lost sister after her death. Several of the Slocum boys who had become businessmen made inquiries about Frances when they traded with indigenous groups—but to no avail.

Half a century and several hundred miles from the time and place of Frances's kidnapping, on the banks of the Mississinewa River near where it spills into the waters of the Wabash, a trader and interpreter named James T. Miller suggested to his companion, Indian agent and merchant Colonel George Washington Ewing, that they seek lodging for the night at the home of a white woman living among the Miami Indians. Ewing had not previously met her. That night two women served dinner, and Ewing talked with one of their husbands; however, it was an elderly woman also at the table who most interested him. He made polite conversation with her in the language of the Miami and was surprised when she signaled that she wished to speak with him after the others fell asleep.

The story that Ewing heard was remarkable. The old woman told him that she was a white woman who had been taken from her family by Indians. Her memories were distant and few, but in six decades she had not forgotten her name, or the image of her father in his broad-brimmed hat, or the family's big house by the Susquehanna River. She also remembered small details about her siblings. Her Miami name was Maconaquah, the old woman revealed, but she had been born to a white family as Frances Slocum.

Frances, her face rough and creased from years of living and working outdoors, was not unhappy about her life. An older Indian couple whose own child had died had adopted her when she'd arrived at their camp with Indian raiders. She'd had a happy childhood, moving often with her new family and community to Pennsylvania, Ohio, and Michigan, near the Niagara in Canada, and to Fort Wayne, Indiana. Her Miami husband, Shepoconah, had become war chief at the Osage Village, but when he later lost his hearing, he gave up his position and moved his family 4 miles up the river to a site then known as "the Deaf Man's Village." Her marriage had produced four children, though two sons had died, and she now had three grandchildren.

Frances asked Ewing not to tell anyone about her identity until after her death, because she feared being taken away again—this time from her Miami family. But she wanted to share her story with someone before she died.

The tale was too extraordinary for Ewing to keep secret; he told his mother, who advised him to try to contact the old woman's relatives. The story almost ends there. Ewing wrote down what Slocum had told him and mailed it to Lancaster, Pennsylvania, asking that the letter be delivered to anyone with the surname of Slocum. Postmaster Mary Dickinson thought it was a strange piece of mail and put it away. The story was rediscovered two years later when a new postmaster found the lost message and took it to the local newspaper, the *Lancaster Intelligencer.*

The letter was published, and a friend sent a copy of the article to Joseph Slocum, a younger brother of Frances. Though it had been almost sixty years since the kidnapping, the incident had certainly not been forgotten. Jonathan Slocum, Joseph's son, wrote to George Washington Ewing and received a reply in three weeks. Ewing was still in touch with the woman known as Maconaquah. He informed the Slocums that the old woman was healthier than when he had first met her but was uncertain how much longer she would live.

Joseph Slocum contacted his other living siblings who were elsewhere in Ohio—brother Isaac and sister Mary Towne. Could Maconaquah be the sibling they had missed all these years? Joseph traveled to Ohio and the three, all in their sixties, set out for the Miami Indian village near present-day Peru, Indiana.

Upon their arrival, Mary rested while the brothers explored the town and contacted merchant James Miller, who left two Miami women tending his store while he met the Slocums at their hotel. When Miller met Joseph and Isaac Slocum, he immediately connected them to Frances, seeing a strong family resemblance. According to Miller, the two Indians he had entrusted with the store were the daughters of Frances Slocum, whom he of course knew as Maconaquah. Miller told Frances's daughters the identity of the town visitors, and the women were immediately afraid. Would these men take their mother? Miller assured them that the Slocums wanted only to be reunited with their lost sister. Miller took the Slocum brothers to the village to see Frances. After sixty years, Frances no longer spoke English and was skeptical that the men were her brothers; other white people had previously tried to claim they were her long-lost family. But Joseph and Isaac told Frances that they recognized her by her missing fingertip. Soon Frances warmed to the men, inviting them into her home. The evening hours found them sitting on a bench in the comfortable log cabin, communicating as best they could; Miller found them still there in the morning.

Through an interpreter, most likely James Miller, Frances described her life among the Delaware and the Miami people. She had distant memories of her abduction, though she did not like to talk about the incident. She remembered other children who were taken from neighboring farms in Pennsylvania; two of them, she recalled with sadness, had been killed because they had cried constantly. Eventually, Frances learned the language of her captors and was given the Delaware name Weletawash.

The Slocums wanted their sister to return east with them for a visit with extended family, but Frances was reluctant. She had told her husband before he died that she would not leave her Indian family and friends. She wouldn't know how to behave, she told her brothers, if she wasn't among the Miami:

> I am an old tree. I cannot move about; I was a young sapling when they took me away. It is all gone past. I am afraid I should die and never come back. I am happy here. I shall die here and lie in that graveyard, and they will raise the pole at my grave, with the white flag on it, and the Great Spirit will know where to find me.

Frances did travel to the hotel in Peru, Indiana, where her sister Mary waited. Her daughters and son-in-law accompanied Frances, bringing deer meat as a gift for the Slocums. The first visit was brief; Mary was emotional and Frances was cool toward the Slocums. But the next day, Frances and her children returned, and they stayed for three days—talking, walking, and eating together. Frances did not want to talk very much about her capture, but the Slocums related their long search for her. After the reunion, they all returned to their homes.

Two years later, Joseph Slocum and his daughters Hannah and Harriet returned to the Peru area—a twenty-three day trip from Pennsylvania—and the woman they knew as Aunt Frances, along with her daughters, gladly welcomed them. Frances hosted them in her log cabin, which stood on 640 acres of land granted to her daughters as part of a government agreement. The family had hogs, cattle, geese, and chickens.

One of Joseph's daughters kept a diary of the trip, writing about Frances:

> She is of small stature, not very much bent, had her hair clubbed behind in calico, tied with worsted ferret; her hair is somewhat gray; her eyes a bright chestnut, clear and sprightly for one of her age; her face is very much wrinkled and weatherbeaten. She has a scar on her left cheek received at an Indian dance; her skin is not as dark as you would expect from her age and constant exposure; her teeth are remarkably good. Her dress was a blue calico short gown, a white Mackinaw blanket, somewhat soiled by constant wear; a fold of blue broadcloth lapped around her, red cloth leggins and buckskin moccasins. The interior of her hut seemed well supplied with all the necessaries, if not with luxuries.

Apparently, Frances had taught her daughters something of the way in which white families prepared dinner. Her niece wrote in her journal:

> They spread the table with a white cotton cloth, and wiped the dishes, as they took them from the cupboard, with a clean cloth. They prepared an excellent dinner of fried venison, potatoes, shortcake, and coffee. Their cups and saucers were small, and they put three or four tablespoonfuls of maple sugar in a cup. The eldest daughter waited on the table, while her mother sat at the table and ate with her white relations. After dinner they washed the dishes, and replaced them upon the shelves, and then swept the floor.

One daughter's name was Kekenokeshwa, meaning "cut finger," because she was the eldest daughter of Maconaquah (who was known to have part of her finger missing); her English name was Nancy Brouillette. At the time of the reunion, she was thirty-six years old.

The younger daughter's name was Ozahshinquah, meaning "yellow leaf," and her English name was Jane. She was then around twenty-four years old and had been married three times, to Indians who were not good husbands. She had three daughters, whose names in English meant "Corn Tassel," "Blue Corn," and "Young Panther." They were later known as Eliza, Frances, and Elizabeth.

George Slocum, the son of Frances's brother Isaac, visited Frances and her daughters in 1845. They all got along so well that Frances asked him to come and live with them; she had asked the same of Joseph Slocum five years before, but he had felt he was too old to move from Pennsylvania. The following year, George brought his wife and two young daughters from Bellevue, Ohio, to live near Frances and her Miami family. He would come to hear much more about her life, including information about her marriages. She told him:

> My father was a Delaware and thought I should marry a Delaware. This Indian came and wanted me to be his wife. He looked all right, but my father was not sure that he would do. So he said, "Do you love this squaw?" "Yes I do," said he. "Then take her and be good to her," my father said. So I went with him back to his wigwam and tried to be a good wife, but he was mean to me. So I went back to my father, for I had a good home there. Then my Delaware husband came and promised me he would be very good to me and I went with him again. But he was still mean and I would not stay with him any longer. I went back to my Indian parents and stayed. He came once more but my father drove him away. I never saw him again. He must have gone into battle and been killed.

Tensions between white settlers and native groups in the region had been escalating as Frances, known as Weletawash by the Delaware, was growing into womanhood. She felt the tension of being a white woman among the Indians, but they continued to accept her. After a particularly difficult conflict between Indian groups and an army general, Frances's adopted family stayed near Kekionga, which the white people called Fort Wayne, Indiana. Then they were on the move again, back east to Ohio. It was there that she met Shepoconah, a Miami Indian chief.

> One day when my parents and I were going down the river we came upon a place where there had been much fighting and many were dead. We saw one young man who was dressed like a chief. He was wounded badly. We wanted to help him and did what we could to heal his wounds. He stayed with us until he

was well. During this time he and I spent many hours together. He was of the Miamis and my Indian parents were of the Delawares. I learned much about his people. He told me how great they had been. I came to love him but was slow to tell my parents. They, too, thought much of him. He had brought us much food from Fort Wayne in the winter time. When he felt he must return to his people my Indian father told him that he would give me to him for his wife. This pleased Shepoconah very much, for that was his name. And so we were married according to Indian fashion. Not much was said or done about it. This agreement was made between Shepoconah and my parents and we were married.

Frances and Shepoconah went back to Fort Wayne to live. When her parents died, the Miami Indians became her people. Though the Delawares had called her Weletawash, the Miamis named her Maconaquah, because she was a "strong little bear woman" who went hunting with her husband and tamed ponies no one else could handle.

Shepoconah and Maconaquah moved with their first-born daughter to the other side of the Mississinewa River, having found a place to live that offered a strong-running spring. Their home became a stopping place for many travelers. Two sons were born, though their lives were short, and another daughter joined the family as well. The family grew corn, squash, and fruits, and raised ponies; they still went hunting, though less frequently, as Shepoconah was growing older and had become deaf. Maconaquah had lived a peaceful, if hardworking, life.

Frances told the Slocums, "The Indians knew I was a white woman. Some of the traders knew that I was, but they did not know where I came from. I was not the only white woman among the Indians, and most of them did not pay much attention to me."

Frances did cross back into the white world—on behalf of her Indian family. In 1840 the Miamis were made to give up their land in northern Indiana and move west; the U.S. government gave the Indian group five years to comply. Frances did not want to move and asked her white brothers for advice. They encouraged her to appeal to Congress as a white woman, not as an Indian. In January 1845 Frances asked the U.S. government for special consideration so she did not have to relocate like the other Miamis, arguing that she and her offspring should be allowed to continue to live on a section of land granted to them in an 1838 treaty. Congressmen from both Indiana and Pennsylvania, the state from which she had been abducted, supported her petition, and the U.S. Congress granted her request.

George Slocum, the nephew who had brought his family to live with Frances near Logansport, Indiana, tried to talk with Frances about Christianity. He would later recall that Frances "believed in a Great Spirit who had given them blessings while they lived and would reward them" in the afterlife. "It was this Good Spirit that caused the maple trees to give sweet water to the Indian for making syrup and sugar. The same spirit caused the corn to grow and bring forth good ears."

In 1847, around six months after George moved to Indiana from Ohio, Frances participated in an all-night dance as part of a thanksgiving celebration. She was seventy-six years old. Afterward, she became ill. She died on March 9, 1847, at her home on the Mississinewa River. Following a Christian burial directed by George, she was buried with a brass kettle and a cream pitcher next to her husband and sons in the Indian cemetery near her home. A pole with a white flag was raised over her grave so "the Great Spirit would know where she was."

RHODA M. COFFIN

1826-1909

Quaker Crusader

RHODA COFFIN STOOD IN FRONT OF Indianapolis's new prison dormitory for women, waiting for its first occupants to arrive. Standing next to her was Sarah Smith, conspicuously dressed in the traditional "Quaker costume" of the time. Smith was to be the matron in charge of the building's new tenants.

Later, Rhoda would remember a "peculiar sensation" as she and Smith prepared to meet the women who would soon arrive from the Indiana state prison in Jeffersonville. She would later recall that they were the "most hardened, debased, and undisciplined of women, scarcely a vestige of womanly instinct among them." Having made reports to the governor and having lobbied the Indiana legislature to reform the inhumane conditions in women's prisons, Rhoda felt responsible for the female inmates who would occupy the new Indiana Reformatory Institute for Women and Girls in Indianapolis.

With values rooted in her Quaker upbringing and faith, Rhoda's belief that female criminals could be rehabilitated was resulting in groundbreaking prison reform in Indiana.

Rhoda M. Johnson was born on February 1, 1826, near Paintersville, Ohio, the fourth child in a strict Quaker family. John and Judith Johnson obeyed the laws of their church, which at that time were exacting—Rhoda later described it as "the straight and narrow"—and raised their children accordingly. The family kept the traditions of silent prayer, dressing in a plain clothing, maintaining a sense of separateness from others, and stressing the necessity of submitting to God's will.

In early childhood, Rhoda loved the freedom of exploring the outdoors and following her father as he worked. She later wrote, "I loved to go with him when he was dropping the corn. He would take two rows, and give me one, then stepping over and helping me with mine, he talked with me and explained different things in which he saw I was interested. Thus he taught me habits of observation."

When Rhoda was old enough to take responsibility for household work, her mother needed her to care for her siblings, run errands, and do other chores. She washed dishes while standing at the sink, perched on a bench her father had made especially for her. She recalled, "The family was large, and reliable female service could not be procured. I entered on new duties and learned new lessons, but the free life I had led suited my inclination better." Her mother modeled "all kinds of work that it was needful for a woman to know."

When Rhoda was sixteen years old, she traveled in a two-horse carriage to Richmond, Indiana, to attend the Indiana Yearly Meeting of Friends, a large regional church meeting. While staying at a hotel en route, she first met her brother's friend Charles Coffin, whose father was a respected Richmond banker. Coffin would one day be her husband, but at the time, Rhoda's mind was on her education, not marriage.

She later wrote, "I was very anxious to have a better education, had strong aspirations to do for myself, to choose some means of livelihood, some independent course of action. There were then no

RHODA M. COFFIN

avenues open for women but household service, sewing, or teaching. My mind was on the latter."

Educational opportunities for young women were limited in the Midwest at the time. Yet in the fall of 1845, Rhoda found a way to pursue further education despite her family's close protection and her father's failing health. The Johnsons agreed that after Rhoda traveled with her brother Brooks and sister-in-law Lydia to the next Indiana Yearly Meeting, she could try to find room and board in Richmond in order to enroll at the Whitewater Monthly Meeting School, held in the Friends' Schoolhouse. When Brooks and Lydia returned home to Ohio, Rhoda wasn't with them.

Though the boardinghouse where she lived was filled with other young people, Rhoda was focused on her studies and paid little attention to anything else. Even when she received multiple offers of marriage from suitors her parents accepted, Rhoda held out for someone who would live up to her ideal. She soon found it in the young man she had met several years earlier, Charles Coffin.

In 1846 Rhoda learned that her father's health was in serious decline, and she returned home. Charles accompanied her, and John Johnson approved the couple's engagement before his death in June. The family farm had to be sold, and Rhoda stayed on to help her widowed mother. In the spring of 1847, Rhoda and Charles were married.

After their wedding at the Friends' meetinghouse in Waynesville, Indiana, Rhoda and Charles made their home in Richmond. The young couple soon settled into a routine, which began when they awoke at five o'clock in the morning and put the teakettle on the stove. Charles would bring in wood and tend the garden, while Rhoda made breakfast. While Charles worked at the bank, Rhoda often occupied her time with sewing for her mother-in-law. She also spent hours reading the Bible and discovered that she did not always agree with church-approved theological commentaries, reflecting later that she was not one to "receive without question" all of the opinions or explanations of Quaker leaders or other theologians.

Married to a man from a prominent family who came from a well-to-do background, Rhoda was in a natural position to have a prominent voice in the Quaker community. She had come to view the church as too strict and its dress code too stifling; she also didn't agree with admonishments from Quaker leaders to stay away from other religious groups, traditional forms of "quiet worship," and the controlling governance of the church.

"The soul longed for liberty but there was none," she later wrote in her memoirs. "I must need follow on as our fathers had done or there was no possible chance for usefulness in the Church. The going outside of it for work was not to be thought of. I honestly tried to walk as they directed, and to dress as they thought I should dress, but it was all an utter failure."

Rhoda and other Orthodox Quakers who felt similarly about the church supported a movement rooted in the ideas of Joseph John Gurney, a Quaker banker from England whose evangelical preaching focused on the importance of scripture, education, and benevolent works and reform outside the Society. He encouraged Quakers to join with other Christians and reformers to promote the greater good—to work for temperance, the abolishment of slavery, and prison reform.

The Coffin family was interested in doing charitable work beyond Quaker circles. In 1835 Elijah Coffin, Charles's father, had started the first Friends' Sabbath School to serve the region, though many Orthodox Quakers objected to its evangelical roots and connections to the world beyond the Society of Friends. In coordination with the American Bible Society, Rhoda joined Elijah and Charles in distributing Bibles to homes in Richmond.

Meanwhile, Rhoda and Charles were starting their own family: Elijah was born in 1848, Charles in 1851, Francis in 1853,

William in 1856, and Mary in 1858. Rhoda and Charles were partners in charitable projects and became leaders in Richmond's Benevolent Society, founded in 1858 as the first interdenominational community organization focused on providing assistance to poor people.

In 1860 Rhoda and Charles requested permission from church elders to organize a prayer event for youth at the Indiana Yearly Meeting. The event attracted more than 2,000 participants who embraced the opportunity to pray without fear of disciplining by traditional-minded elders. To continue to provide young people with this type of worship environment, the Coffins hosted a weekly prayer group in their home. For Rhoda, this was a liberating and energizing way of feeding her faith. It launched the true beginning of her "benevolent career."

The 1860s were active times for women's societies that had formed to aid the wounded and destitute following the Civil War. The population was growing in Richmond, and so was the poverty level of its residents. Rhoda and a group of women Friends organized and went from home to home to assess neediness and to offer spiritual guidance. They decided to create a mission school for poor children.

Obtaining financial help from Charles, Rhoda and her women's group received permission to make use of an abandoned public school building. In the spring of 1864, they enrolled 30 students and began teaching the "right standard of living." One year later, the ecumenical school—Marion Street Sabbath School—had grown to serve 250 students, and Charles and Rhoda Coffin were made its joint superintendents. The couple placed updates about the school in articles published in local newspapers.

Rhoda—an upper-class, Protestant banker's wife—had a very different life than those who received her Christian charity. As members of top social circles in Richmond and Indianapolis, the

Coffins maintained a large home staffed with domestic servants and filled with top-quality items. The family was largely removed from the kinds of personal hardship that were a daily reality for those less fortunate in education, wealth, and society. But Rhoda would continue to learn about ways to enact social change through her leadership in the Quaker community. While she was not the most radical reform-minded woman in Richmond, Rhoda Coffin felt that the "energy of Quaker women needed to be harnessed for reform efforts." In 1866 she joined in forming the Home Mission Association (HMA) to unite Orthodox Quaker women around the issue of gaining a voice in the Church. When a female Quaker minister from Michigan withdrew from leadership of the HMA because she feared sanctioning from Friends' Meeting elders, Rhoda organized an HMA gathering that drew 700 women who then elected Rhoda as the group's president. In addition to holding local weekly prayer meetings, the group circulated tracts on religious themes, started Sunday school programs, and made visits to jails.

In 1868 HMA established the Home for Friendless Women as a service to poor single mothers, homeless women, and children who were illegitimate or who suffered from birth defects or disease. While the law required that men, not women, serve as trustees of the board, Rhoda served as its manager and learned new leadership skills. She sought broader support for the organization by working with the local newspaper in sharing the stories of the home's residents.

It was through their work as superintendents of the Marion Street Sabbath School that Rhoda and Charles were brought into further contact with fellow, albeit less-fortunate, Indiana citizens. They began to observe that a number of the students, mostly boys, had little supervision from parents or other responsible adults. This seemed to the Coffins to be contributing to the city's growing crime rate. The increasingly influential couple lobbied Indiana Governor Oliver Morton to convince him of the need for a state reform institution for boys that focused on education and discipline. Governor Morton created a commission to examine the issue, and the result was the establishment of the House of Refuge for Juvenile Offenders. Charles was named to the board of managers for the House, which was located in Plainfield, Indiana.

In 1868 new Indiana Governor Conrad Baker asked Charles and Rhoda to visit the state's two penitentiaries and report on prison conditions. Despite their benevolent work, the couple was ill equipped for the impact of the visit. Both male and female prisoners said they had been sexually abused; guards bribed imprisoned women for favors and forced the women to bathe in front of them. The Coffins shared their findings with the governor, who visited the state prisons himself and made recommendations to the wardens for improving conditions.

But the Coffins felt that the revised policies didn't go far enough to protect female inmates from abuse. Rhoda began to develop a passion for prison reform. She felt that women imprisoned for their crimes could be successfully rehabilitated. She advocated for placing the state's male and female convicts in separate prisons and for the women's institution to be run by women—believing that women were best equipped to understand the needs of female inmates.

The Indiana legislature passed a bill in 1869 to establish the Indiana Reformatory Institute for Women and Girls. It would be built in Indianapolis. In addition to having a female warden (and a traditional Quaker one at that), the inmates transferred to the new facility were to be taught housekeeping and sewing skills. Rhoda felt it was valuable for the prisoners to have work to do during their incarceration.

There was, however, still one part of the legislative bill of 1869 that Rhoda wanted to change. The new institute was still financially controlled by an all-male management board. In 1876 Rhoda became the first woman to speak to the National Prison Congress. Her speech that advocated for women's prisons to be staffed only by females was met with hearty approval.

The following year, a committee of the state senate discovered that the budget of the Reformatory Institute for Women and Girls had poor oversight, and that the superintendent and the board were frequently in conflict. The legislature passed a bill creating an all-female board for the institute, and the governor named Rhoda Coffin to the board. She soon became the board's president and the institute's budget was balanced within a few years.

As the first prison to be run entirely by women, the Indiana Reformatory Institute for Women and Girls was closely watched; opponents were certain it would fail. Instead, the institute became a benchmark for prison reform—across the state and the nation. Now considered an expert on prisons for women, Rhoda was frequently asked to write and speak about her experiences, with a focus on reform.

Rhoda's upper-class, evangelical Christian background dictated that she often take a behind-the-scenes role in support of her husband's benevolent activities, although the Coffins continued to work together in supporting shared causes. Rhoda remained convinced that women could make a difference in society by applying their morals to good works; she also began to find hope in political avenues.

Nearing her fifties, Rhoda was attracted to a new cause: the Women's Crusade. Rhoda and a group of other prominent American women of British heritage waged war on the saloons of Richmond, preaching about the evils of alcohol. But German immigrants, who felt that alcohol was part of their cultural tradition, fought back. The Women's Crusade was accused of being ethnically prejudiced and of stepping beyond their proper role as nineteenth-century women.

In March of 1874 Rhoda told a local newspaper reporter that she had "not sinned for three years" and "enjoyed the smiles of Jesus." These comments were perceived as self-righteous, and newspaper articles that followed questioned her "presumptuous" statement. The work of the Crusade fell out of favor, and, in the next election, so did the local Republican ticket that had supported it. Soon the evangelical movement lost its influence. Rhoda and other Richmond women decided to embrace a more traditional organization, and in November of 1874, they launched a local chapter of the Women's Christian Temperance Union.

In 1880 Rhoda again picked up reform work on behalf of institutionalized women—this time, though, the institution was not a prison but an asylum. She wanted women in the asylum to benefit from having a female doctor. Rhoda began to see these mental health-care needs as women's rights issues. "I came out of that contest a full-fledged woman suffragist. If a vote was necessary before I could succeed in getting a woman physician to care for the helpless of my sex, I decided that I must have a vote," she said. She never joined formal suffrage organizations, however.

As society changed and Rhoda grew older, her political capital began to decline in Richmond circles. After she faced opposition to her role as president of the board of the Indiana Reformatory, she resigned the post. But a more difficult trial was to come when, in 1894, Charles Coffin's bank went into financial collapse. Not only did the family lose most of its fortune, but they also lost the confidence of their Richmond neighbors. The Coffins claimed that a business panic had caused the bank to fail, but they nevertheless received threats on their lives. The family decided to leave their longtime home and move to Chicago.

Though the Coffins' reputation for visionary reform work was tarnished by the bank scandal, Rhoda continued to write and speak about the need to transform America's prisons. In 1894 she visited Chicago-area prisons and insane asylums and addressed the National Prison Association.

Moving beyond benevolent work on behalf of the institutionalized, she became involved with the Protective Agency for Women and Children, which sought legislation to grant property rights to women and general rights to children—an issue also being addressed by suffragists. She also wanted state schools to explicitly teach Christian values.

Rhoda only became less active in public issues when her health began to decline. She seemed to accept the disadvantages of aging, satisfied that the energy she had applied to her reform work, including groundbreaking prison reform initiatives, had been worthwhile. While she had stepped beyond the typical roles for women, she had continued to hold strong convictions about the positive moral influence of women in their families and society.

According to her husband in the last months of her life, Rhoda's body was weak but her mind was clear and strong. She was able to attend regular Quaker Meetings in Chicago, offering prayer and ministering words to members of the Society who respected her and sought her advice. "She had remarkably good judgment and a strong mind, and was able to give helpful advice to those who were in trouble or sorrow of any kind," Charles wrote.

The last Meeting Rhoda attended was on September 5, 1909. She offered a community prayer and then asked for the gathering of Quakers to sing the hymn, "Nearer My God to Thee."

Rhoda died on September 28, 1909, with Charles and family friends at her side at their Chicago home. Her funeral was held in Richmond, and, despite the difficult circumstances under which they had left the town, many people attended the service.

In a remembrance, Mary Coffin Johnson wrote:

Christian activity was the strong element in her nature . . . she consecrated herself to bear the standard of the Lord in *practical* service, and soon pressed forward for the betterment of those in lowly condition, the fallen and the outcast. She was not an idealist; her devising and shaping of methods, aided by earnest co-workers "in all their degrees," developed into practical things accomplished. . . . She was optimistic in temperament, one who met life's tasks with good cheer, looking steadily at its hopeful side. . . . She may sometimes have seemed radical in the advocacy of her policies and made mistakes, or been misunderstood, for her resourceful nature, her strong mentality and alert energy. . . . The works, ranging over a wide horizon, in which she took prominent part, are followed to-day with material benefits to the world.

MAY WRIGHT SEWALL

1844-1920

Women's Suffragist and Peace Activist

How was the suffragist spirit ignited for Indiana women?

For May Wright Sewall, an important moment came when she was a young, energetic high school teacher in Indianapolis. A distinguished community leader named Zerelda Wallace, president of the state chapter of the Women's Christian Temperance Union, presented May with a petition in favor of temperance—making alcohol illegal—to be sent to the Indiana General Assembly. Ever the teacher, May took time to carefully read the document and found a phrase that stopped her cold: It declared that those who signed the petition in favor of temperance would not "clamor" for other civil or political rights.

Said May, "But I do clamor!" She declined to sign the petition. May later expressed her distress at seeing "one more proof of the degree to which honorable women love to humiliate themselves before men for sweet favor's sake." Though May was angry about this incident and about the fact that the legislature ignored the temperance petition, she would later work with Wallace, the widow of Governor David Wallace, to form the Indianapolis Equal Suffrage Society.

The focus of the society included rights for women, which would be debated in Indiana for decades. The exposure would bring May into contact with the country's leading suffragists and would ignite a passion for justice in her that would expand from state to national, and even international, concerns.

Mary—who later gave herself the name "May"—Wright was born in the Honey Creek settlement near Greenfield, Wisconsin, on May 27, 1844, the second daughter and youngest of four children of Philander Montague and Mary Wright. Her father was a Harvard University graduate who had taught school and then turned to farming.

May was choosing books to read from her father's library by the age of seven. The family knew that Philander wanted his daughter to follow in his footsteps and attend an Ivy League university, even though girls of that era were not generally encouraged to pursue higher education. May's father told her that women should have the same opportunities as men. Later, May would also credit her father for instilling in her a sense of justice for the rights of all human beings.

Though she did not go east to a university, May wanted to get a good education. To save for her studies, she took charge of a one-room schoolhouse in Waukesha, Wisconsin, in 1863. By becoming a teacher, she started down a vocational path that she would continue for years to come.

In 1865 May attended Northwestern Female College in Evanston, Illinois, for one year, taking courses in chemistry, Latin, logic, rhetoric, trigonometry, and zoology. She received a diploma and went on to teach in Wisconsin and Michigan. Her salary each semester was just under $100.

In 1871 May accepted a position teaching German at the high school in Franklin, Indiana. When the academic year was over, she returned to Michigan and, on March 2, 1872, married Edwin W. Thompson, a mathematics teacher. Edwin—a thin, graceful man

MAY WRIGHT SEWALL

with a dark complexion, brown eyes, and wavy hair—was twenty-four when he and May were married; she was twenty-seven.

In 1873 May returned to the Franklin high school as principal and Edwin became superintendent of schools. The couple then moved to Indianapolis and took teaching positions, May again giving instruction in German and Edwin joining the business department at Indianapolis High School.

The couple had been married only a short time when Edwin died of tuberculosis in 1875. In spite of her grief, May was kept busy, putting her energy into teaching and community activities, like helping to start the Indianapolis Women's Club.

Three years later, Indianapolis social circles were abuzz about a possible meeting of women who had ideas beyond the scope of typical "club women." Responding to a secret invitation, nine women and one man met in the city's Circle Hall to talk about their interest in organizing to advocate for women's rights.

Indiana—the country's nineteenth state—had been deliberating issues surrounding rights for women since 1850. The state was home to one of the first women's suffrage organizations in the United States, but prevailing opinion in the relatively conservative city of Indianapolis was that equal-rights legislation would be "radical at best." May later said of the gathering, "Had we convened consciously to plot the ruin of our domestic life, which opponents predict as the result of woman's enfranchisement, we could not have looked more guilty or have moved about with more unnatural stealth."

A month later the group met again and its size was doubled. The result of this second meeting was the founding of the Indianapolis Equal Suffrage Society, open to both genders for membership. The society's mission was to achieve "equal rights at the ballot box for all citizens on the same conditions."

The group was very active in the next decade. In addition to holding forty-three public hearings and distributing thousands of tracts, the group attracted regional attention by sponsoring visiting lectures from nationally known equal-rights advocates Susan B. Anthony, Elizabeth Cady Stanton, and Frances Willard. Ready to take a more visible leadership role, May was elected secretary of the organization; Zerelda Wallace became its president.

Around the same time, May became acquainted with Theodore Lovett Sewall, a Harvard University graduate who had settled in Indianapolis in the summer of 1876 and started the respected Classical School for Boys. The two met at a Unitarian church. A friend of May's recalled "seeing him go forward" to meet Thompson "as she approached, he looking very tall and slim in a Prince Albert and a silk hat and she radiant in a brown silk dress made with an overskirt, and a bonnet that tied under her chin with a pink ribbon."

In October of 1880 the couple married. Theodore held progressive views about the status of women, and May felt she'd found a perfect match. "Marriage is the natural condition," she said to a reporter, "but I believe in woman living her own life and working out her own salvation in her own way." A few months later, in December, the Indianapolis Equal Suffrage Society delivered letters to each state legislator—as well as to Indiana's top newspapers— stating that the organization was preparing to ask the Indiana General Assembly to pass a bill that would allow women to vote in presidential elections. They were also asking them to amend the state constitution to grant women the right to vote in all elections.

While their effort to influence the state to pass the first bill failed after two readings at the Fifty-second Indiana General Assembly in January 1881, the group was more successful in lobbying the legislature to vote on an amendment that would allow Hoosier women the right to vote in all elections. The resolution passed in the state house of representatives by a 62-to-24 vote on April 7, 1881; one day later, the state senate also approved it, by a vote of 27 to 18. With this victory came the Indiana constitution's next requirement that the amendment would still have to be passed by two consecutive legislative bodies and only then sent to statewide vote. The suffragists organized meetings and lectures and distributed literature, working to gain support for a vote that wouldn't be considered again for two years.

In November 1881 the *Indianapolis Times* gave its support to women's suffrage. "As the question is likely to become a prominent theme of discussion," the newspaper editorialized, "the *Times* will now say that it is decidedly and unequivocally in favor of woman suffrage. We believe that women have the same right to vote that men have, that it is impolitic and unjust to deprive them of the right, and that its free and full bestowal would conserve the welfare of society and the good of government." The *Times* also gave the suffragists the opportunity to reach a broad, public audience through a weekly newspaper column, which May Sewall wrote and edited for the next four years. Under the title "Women's Work," May covered issues set forth by the Indianapolis Equal Suffrage Society, such as women working outside the home, the potential for women earning wages equal to men, and opportunities in higher education.

On May 19, 1882, the state association of suffragists, led by May, held a forum at the Grand Opera House in Indianapolis for all Indiana women interested in having the right-to-vote amendment passed. More than 5,000 Hoosier women sent postcards of support. However, in January 1883 the amendment was defeated by the Fifty-third Indiana General Assembly.

In her professional life, May and her husband Theodore opened the Girls' Classical School of Indianapolis, an equal counterpart to the excellent educational opportunity boys received at the Indianapolis Classical School. Where the Indianapolis Female School and Miss Hooker's Female School taught subjects like music, painting, and drawing that were considered proper for society girls, the

Girls' Classical School patterned itself after "leading New England Academies."

May, who taught literature, was known for her strictness. One student would later recall, "There was no nonsense about Mrs. Sewall . . . She looked through a large magnifying glass which enlarged her eye," not unlike "a Cyclops of most forbidding appearance." She also initiated a dress code for her students that emphasized simplicity and comfort; rather than the tiny, corseted waists of women's Victorian-era clothing, May insisted on attire that allowed for freedom of movement. This was important, since she encouraged physical training, something very unusual for girls at that time. A newspaper reporter who visited the school was impressed by Sewall's program for academic and physical education, writing in the *Indianapolis News* that a "spirit of happiness is suffused through the school." The senior class of women was especially impressive, the reporter wrote. "They are not the kind of girls who lose their temper and self-possession under difficulties. They are not the sort of person who screams at trifles, nor do they call everything 'lovely'— cabbages, waterfalls and all—and they are not the ones who wear shoes a great deal too small when they are young, and require shoes a great deal too large when they are old. They appear permanently well poised, mentally and bodily."

May and Theodore Sewall gave their support to the newly forming Art Association of Indianapolis in 1883. May then helped organize the Western Association of Collegiate Alumnae, serving as president in 1886 and 1888. This group was later incorporated into the American Association of University Women.

May's dedication to the cause of women's rights continued, and she served as chair of the executive committee of the National Woman Suffrage Association. While Lucretia Mott, Elizabeth Stanton, and Susan B. Anthony represented the first wave of suffragists—the "old guard"—May and her contemporaries represented a new generation.

A May 3, 1887, article in the *Indianapolis Journal* noted that Mrs. Sewall spoke at the Indiana Woman Suffrage Convention held at the Grand Opera House. She discussed the four-decade history of the suffrage movement, as well as innovative initiatives such as working with libraries to encourage the addition of historical documentation about women's suffrage to their collections and talking with religious leaders to "enlighten them about the history of the movement thus far." Following Sewall on the program was Susan B. Anthony. The next year, the two women together signed an open letter, published in state newspapers, to General Benjamin Harrison—who had been nominated to the Republican presidential ticket—about the factual basis for their movement to give women the right to vote. They noted, for example, that women were considered "lawful citizens," as evidenced by the fact that they were asked to pay taxes and were recognized in public courts as citizens.

In 1887 the Indianapolis Equal Suffrage Society restructured and expanded into a state organization tied to the National Woman Suffrage Association. In 1888 May and Frances Willard made arrangements to hold a convention in Washington, D.C., to celebrate the fortieth anniversary of the Seneca Falls Convention—the historic meeting of early women's rights leaders in New York. Interest in forming two new groups emerged from this gathering: the National Council of Women, for which May served as recording secretary and later president, and the International Council of Women (ICW). A resolution passed at the convention stipulated that the first International Council of Women meeting would be held in 1893 at the World's Columbian Exhibition in Chicago. Charles C. Bonney, president of the World's Congress Auxiliary, consented to this with the understanding that it would be called the World's Congress of Representative Women at the Chicago exhibition.

May's commitment to expanding a national, and then international, coalition of women's groups was a major force behind the organization of the National Council of Women in the United States and, eventually, the International Council of Women. The purpose was to bring together women from different countries and cultures, "committed to different interests in order that they may demonstrate to one another how far their resemblances transcend their differences and to what degree they are capable of uniting in the accomplishment of a common unselfish purpose."

May also traveled throughout Europe in an effort to gather support for the World's Congress of Representative Women. This began a new chapter in her life, when she would work to bring together women of different countries and diverse economic and social classes to address women's concerns. She was progressive in her thinking about issues of suffrage, internationalism, and the role of American women as global leaders.

May believed it was important for "club women" to be concerned about females outside of their own class or social, religious, and political interests. They "were equally related to larger interests: that indeed the likenesses existing among the most different classes of women were larger than the differences among the same classes." Even as she was taking up the concerns of the world's women, May had to face a personal difficulty close to home. On December 23, 1895, she was widowed once again when Theodore Sewall died of tuberculosis. She assumed the principalship of the Girls' Classical School and began expanding its programs to offer classes for adults. But immersing herself in her work did not erase the pain of her loss. Some of her friends and acquaintances were taken aback when she began taking an interest in spiritualism—a growing movement that, though of questionable validity, particularly drew in those with loved ones who had died.

Still May continued to be concerned with worldly issues, which helped her focus on something beyond her immediate grief. May served as president of the ICW from 1899 to 1904, leading five million women in eleven countries. The ICW's main opportunity for visibility was its yearly executive meetings, where they actively promoted peace. May was particularly interested in reforms that would foster greater understanding between countries and cultures. Bringing her perspective as an educator to the ICW, May urged all member countries to reexamine their school texts in order to de-emphasize military achievement. After all, she felt, what good were international peace talks if nothing would be done to "abate the mutual ignorance and consequent dislike, not to say hatred, of the representatives of different races in the different cities in which we live." She encouraged schools in the United States, for example, to focus on the progress of industry through the contributions of hundreds of thousands of immigrants. To further encourage peaceful coexistence, May encouraged mothers worldwide to take away toys from their children that promoted or glorified warfare.

May Sewall retired from directing the Girls' Classical School in 1907, making front-page headlines in the Indianapolis press. In the summer, she left the city to give lectures at Green-Acre-on-the-Piscataqua, in Eliot, Maine, where conferences were held on religion and philosophy. Now an internationally known figure, May was a featured speaker.

Active in retirement, May again applied her gift for organization to chairing the International Conference of Women Workers to Promote Permanent Peace. Though World War I was occupying international energy and attention, May persevered and scheduled the conference for July 1915 in San Francisco. It drew more than 500 delegates from twelve countries. At the conference, the delegates passed resolutions against secret treaties signed between governments, the use of military drills in schools, and the use of public monies in praise of war. The attendees sought the formation of an international lawmaking entity, court, and police force. They wanted political rights for all women, and demanded that nations should agree to disarm and that neutral countries should act as mediators for nations in conflict.

May's work as a peace activist culminated in November 1915, when automaker and industrial leader Henry Ford invited her to join him and sixty other delegates in a civilian mission to end WWI. On the *Oscar II,* the group sailed for Norway, hoping that they would be able to bring soldiers home in time for Christmas. Unfortunately, the group did not succeed. No serious attention was given to their efforts, and the war continued its destructive march across Europe.

In 1918 May met with the well-known author Booth Tarkington, an Indianapolis native and author of *The Magnificent Ambersons,* showing him a manuscript she had written. To Tarkington's surprise, the book was not about her career as an educator or a philosophical exploration of women's suffrage but about her experiences with spiritualism. Sewall, he discovered, had been intrigued by the notion that it was possible for the living to communicate with a spirit world. Calling the manuscript "sincere" and "unique," yet admitting it was "strange," he stated later that he was "astonished to discover that for more than twenty years, this academic-liberal of a thousand human activities . . . had been really living not with the living, so to put it."

Many people in Indianapolis knew May for her work as a formidable educator and suffragette, but few knew about her involvement in spiritualism. Indianapolis was home to May, and upon her return, she moved into a convalescent home because of heart disease and difficulty in breathing. Some of her former students from the Girls' Classical School spent time caring for her.

Because of her poor health, May couldn't participate in the social and political life of Indianapolis as she had in earlier years, but she remained of interest to local media. The *Indianapolis News* interviewed her to ask for her views on a number of topics, including world events and suffrage. Talking about global peace, May said that this admirable goal would only come about through "spiritual reformation, by the movement of the soul, not by the use of ammunition."

May spent her final months making corrections on the galleys of her book, which, thanks largely to Booth Tarkington, found a publisher in the Bobbs-Merrill Company of Indianapolis. *Neither Dead nor Sleeping,* published in May of 1920, revealed May's sincere belief that she had communicated with the dead, including her late husband Theodore. Understandably, there were skeptics; this was a very different image of the educator and organizer known to so many. Though she had been interested in spiritualism for years, May had waited until near the end of her life to share these experiences—perhaps knowing at some level that she would be doubted and not wanting to see other areas of her life's work discounted.

May Sewall died on July 22, 1920. She is remembered as a very effective organizer and reformer who was convinced that the abilities of women and the potential for their positive influence could contribute to the making of a better world.

VIRGINIA CLAYPOOL MEREDITH

1848–1936

Agriculture Queen

AFTER VIRGINIA CLAYPOOL MEREDITH BURIED HER husband of only a dozen years, she had a choice to make. She had been managing the house and family needs of the Meredith family's farm, known nationally for its breeds of sheep and cattle, and now had to decide whether to keep the operation going or to sell the property and livestock and start a different kind of life.

For Virginia the decision was not a difficult one. She was passionate about the place of the farm in society and the dignity of agricultural work and had learned a lot about livestock care and breeding. She wanted to continue to hold large sales events at the farm, enjoying how the breeders and stock owners came from far and wide to buy the Meredith's well-bred animals and incorporate their bloodlines into their own stock.

She would keep Oakland Farm and manage it successfully, in addition to becoming a well-known champion of agriculture. Over time she would come to be called the "Queen of American

Agriculture," in recognition of her multifaceted work in promoting the "privileges and possibilities of farm life."

Virginia Claypool, the firstborn in a line of eight children, was named after the state of Virginia, the birthplace of her pioneering Claypool grandfather. Her father Austin B. Claypool had endured the hardships of a childhood in rough wilderness as he had helped his family carve out a settlement in central Indiana. He had become well educated, and Virginia grew up in a home of civility and culture. The family was also very active in their rural community.

Virginia was twelve years old when the country erupted in Civil War. Austin Claypool did not keep the news of southern secession from his children; he wanted them to understand the struggle that was dividing the young country. The Claypool family was proud when their patriotic daughter loaned her horse to a neighbor who volunteered with the Indiana cavalry; Virginia reportedly said that she gave up the animal in order to do her part in preserving the Union.

In her middle teens, Virginia enrolled at Glendale College near Cincinnati, Ohio, in part to fulfill her father's wish that his sons and daughters be "public spirited." Austin Claypool also wanted his children to be well informed and commanded Virginia to regularly read the *Cincinnati Gazette* and other publications of the day. She took his advice, which began a lifelong habit that would serve her well.

Virginia graduated from Glendale at the age of nineteen and returned home to learn the finer points of homemaking. This would prepare her to start a household when, two years later, she married Henry Clay Meredith, the son of General Solomon Meredith, a respected gentleman farmer in eastern Indiana.

The Merediths owned and operated a 400-acre spread called Oakland Farm, breeding healthy herds of Shorthorn cattle and Southdown sheep. The farm became something of a model operation, with visitors from across the country coming to Indiana to

VIRGINIA CLAYPOOL MEREDITH

learn from the Merediths. When she married into the family, Virginia embraced the role of hostess, and when Henry's mother died, his bride capably took up the responsibilities of directing the busy household.

In addition to the day-to-day work, the farm hosted large public livestock sales, which were major events for the region. Many sellers, buyers, and onlookers experienced Virginia's hospitality. She naturally cultivated her homemaking skills as she managed the family's domestic life.

Virginia's husband died in 1882, several years after his father had passed away. Determined to keep the Meredith farm running, she hired an experienced manager to care for the cattle and sheep. Buyers who came to the farm found that the quality of the stock under Virginia's supervision remained high. Virginia also continued to host the large, popular public sales that had put Oakland Farm on the map.

In addition to the public events at home, Virginia also showed sheep and cattle at farming events and was successful despite the fact that it was very unusual at the time—even unheard of—for a woman to exhibit livestock. She won many prizes for the quality of her Oakland Farm animals.

In the early 1880s Virginia began to accept invitations to give presentations at breeders' conventions, as well as to the State Board of Agriculture. She proved to be a knowledgeable and exceptional speaker, not only on livestock husbandry but also on wide-ranging topics related to homemaking. Virginia had become interested in advancing the idea that homemaking—the work of skillfully organizing and maintaining domestic life—was a calling worthy of respect.

Although Virginia and Henry had not started a family before his untimely death, Virginia would yet experience motherhood. A good friend from Cambridge City fell ill and, on her deathbed, requested that Virginia raise her two children as her own. Virginia graciously complied and took Mary and Meredith Matthews into her busy household. Virginia took on the role of mother with her usual dedication, giving the children plenty of affection and investing in their education.

Virginia was one of the first individuals—man or woman—to be asked by the superintendent of the State Board of Agriculture to serve on the staff of speakers when farmers' institutes were established in 1889. For the next twenty-five years, she was sent across the state to educate Indiana farm families. In each community she visited, she was always warmly received. One description of her presentations said that her "pleasing personality and her musical voice, together with her earnestness and sincerity eventually made her one of the most popular speakers in the state." As her reputation grew, she was invited to other states to speak as well.

In the early 1890s Virginia traveled to Vicksburg, Mississippi, as a guest speaker at an agricultural meeting. At the last session of the meeting, following her final address, she was asked to accept a gold medal with the inscription, "The Citizens of Vicksburg, Mississippi, to the Queen of American Agriculture." Given with all sincerity and honor, the gesture took Virginia by surprise. The new title would follow her throughout her career as a speaker, hostess, advocate, homemaking educator, and leader.

In 1893 Virginia was appointed by the state's agricultural commission to serve as Indiana's representative on the National Board of Lady Managers at the World's Columbian Exposition in Chicago; she was responsible for areas pertaining to women at the fair. She was then asked to serve as chairperson of the committee on awards, which meant that she would be responsible for selecting and overseeing more than one hundred judges from a number of different countries and cultures. This role was time consuming, and Virginia needed to be in Chicago most of the time during the next several years. She returned to Oakland Farm every two weeks to supervise its management. She also managed to keep up a regular speaking schedule during this time.

One of the addresses that Virginia was asked to deliver time and time again was called "Privileges and Possibilities of Farm Life." Speaking specifically to the sons and daughters of farmers, she wanted them to understand that agriculture offered all kinds of career and lifestyle opportunities for intelligent young men and women. She strongly encouraged them to continue the work of their families on the farm rather than move toward the cities for trade or factory work. By honoring the work of farmers, and impressing upon the next generation that the farming vocation was important and meaningful, Virginia helped build a foundation for the future work of 4-H clubs still thriving today.

Virginia's "Privileges and Possibilities of Farm Life" speech was published and distributed in almost every English-speaking country around the world. The final thoughts she shared in that presentation extolled the strength of the farm as a cornerstone of American life and individual health:

> Let us dignify our calling; let us exalt our home on the farm by making it the abode of intelligence, refinement and comfort—the abode of peace. Let us make much of our farm and our farm life, let us cherish its privileges, let us realize its possibilities. The farmer alone, of all men, has a home. . . . The family, that great institution, ordained by the Father, should find nowhere else such congenial conditions for its development. . . . [T]he oak grown in free air weighs twice as much as that grown in the dense shade. May not the boy grown in free air develop more manliness than one dwarfed by the close crowding of other natures?

While Virginia had learned her homemaking skills during her

growing-up years, and as the capable manager and hostess at Oakland Farm, she knew that not all girls gleaned all they needed to know about household caretaking from their mothers. She envisioned a program at Purdue University—the state's land grant college known for its excellent agricultural school—specifically for young women to learn household management skills. She felt that women should be prepared for their "life's role" in their work on the farm. However, Purdue wasn't prepared to launch a department devoted to domestic-life education. The university's faculty and trustees needed to see what such a program would entail. An opportunity at the agricultural school at the University of Minnesota would provide an innovative testing ground. The Minnesota school asked Virginia to establish and direct a new program specifically for girls, to prepare them for their work on their family farms. Believing that she wasn't qualified to create the new program, Virginia turned down the offer, despite her significant experience and advocacy. But the school kept calling, and Virginia was eventually persuaded to accept the post.

In 1896 Virginia started her coordinator position with the College of Agriculture at the University of Minnesota, which was in session six months out of the year. For nearly six years, Virginia gave instruction in the areas in which she had become so knowledgeable. Areas of study included household economics and budgeting, meal planning, shopping, food preparation, sewing, entertaining, cleaning, home safety, caring for children, and more. Her adopted daughter Mary entered the new department as a student and advanced through the program that Virginia had designed.

During this time, Oakland Farm continued to thrive under the care of the expert herdsmen Virginia had hired. She returned to the farm during the months that school was not in session, keeping in touch with her Hoosier agricultural colleagues and the women's groups of Cambridge City with which she was involved.

Virginia was a member of civic organizations in Cambridge City as well as the Indiana Union of Literary Clubs. Active in both, she attended regularly and provided her input in decision making. When the Union of Literary Clubs merged to form the Indiana state federation of clubs, she twice served as president of the consolidated group—the only woman to do so. Much later, in 1918, Virginia would be made honorary president of the Indiana Union of Literary Clubs, and when she made an appearance, its members rose in admiration. The tradition continued until her health in older age prevented her from attending.

Her Indiana community was surprised when, on May 17, 1900, a newspaper story reported that Oakland Farm had been sold. The property had been in the Meredith family for seventy-five years, but Virginia had been offered a premium price. Not to be removed from rural life, she purchased another property south of Cambridge City and called it Narborough Farm. She made that farm her home until 1916.

Beyond her public-speaking engagements, Virginia also worked with a respected weekly livestock journal, the *Breeder's Gazette,* first as an occasional column contributor and then as editor of the "home department." Her section of the publication, filled with her ideas, advice, and encouragement, was popular with readers.

Virginia had a remarkable gift for welcoming people from a range of backgrounds when she entertained them—first at Oakland Farm and then at Narborough Farm. She was considered an equal to the most accomplished women in the state and even the nation and had many contacts through her work with the Columbian Expedition. But she was just as pleased to host farmers and livestock breeders at her home. Whether a visitor was a neighbor with a small farm or a dignitary from another state, Virginia was considered the most hospitable hostess in Indiana.

With evidence of the success of the homemaking curriculum

at the College of Agriculture in Minnesota, administrators at Purdue University were finally prepared to start a program for young women, a counterpart to the agricultural department that educated young men. Purdue had followed Virginia's work in Minnesota and approved of the direction of the program, seeing the validity in the "professionalizing" of domestic education. Virginia's adopted daughter Mary Matthews was appointed as the founding dean of Purdue University's School of Home Economics. Virginia was pleased that Purdue had taken this step and proud of Mary.

In 1913 Virginia was elected as the first president of the Indiana Home Economics Association and was twice reappointed to the role. She was enthusiastically supportive of the Home Economics Association for the rest of her life.

Virginia's sale of Narborough Farm in 1916 was followed by a move to Lafayette, Indiana, where she would be close to Purdue University and her daughter Mary. In 1921 the woman who had so strongly influenced thinking about the role of women in successful home and farm life was recognized by the State of Indiana by being asked to join the Board of Trustees of Purdue University. Virginia Meredith was the first woman to be offered the prestigious appointment. Just as with everything else she undertook in life, she was sensible and more than competent to fulfill this role. She not only held her own among the male-dominated board, she also became an influential member who took special interest in the female students and faculty who were embodying the vision she had long held.

Virginia's attention expanded beyond the agricultural programs for young women and men, however, and she became known for her astuteness in working with the trustees as they grappled with institutional issues. A board tribute later described her as "not only a brilliant woman, of wide interests, with a comprehensive grasp of many difficulties that beset the Board, but she was also a loyal and understanding friend, wise in her counsels, keen but kindly in her criticisms. She was ever alive to world conditions and world problems, yet vitally interested in the home and its influence. She was a delightful hostess in a home which one entered with joy and left with a consciousness of uplift and blessing." Virginia participated in board meetings even as her health failed and she had to give up other interests and commitments. She served on the board for fifteen years.

In 1930 the State of Wisconsin honored her with an award "for eminent service," which had never been bestowed on a woman outside of the state, explaining, "To Virginia Claypool Meredith who, working alone, won success in farming and later, working with others, pioneered effectively in the science of homemaking."

On December 10, 1936, Virginia died at age eighty-eight at her home in Lafayette. The *Lafayette Journal,* in an editorial on December 11 of that year, summed up her life's work in service to agriculture and to the state of Indiana with these concluding words:

> Whether as an aggressive, successful stock-raiser, carrying on the large business of a departed husband; as a messenger to farmers' institutes, passing on her own experiences to men and women; as an orator contacting groups in many states; as an educator establishing new ideas and modern methods, or as the distinguished trustee of a university, Mrs. Meredith was ever a valued contributor to the public good. She had very definite ideas as to the aims and functions of Purdue University as a sound factor in the education of young womanhood for homemaking.
>
> Keen of wit, zestful, humorous, quick at repartee, sure in decision as between right and wrong, courageous and frank in support of her convictions, Mrs. Meredith combined in one vibrant and friendly personality those myriad qualities that make for leadership.

Neither titles nor medals of precious worth, nor the applause of thrilled multitudes may express with any measure of adequacy the significance or extent of the great service she rendered to her state, to Purdue University and to those who were fortunate to know her as friend and counselor.

ELIZA ANN COOPER BLAKER

1854-1926

Early Childhood Pioneer

To visit one of the Free Kindergarten Society classrooms in Indianapolis at the beginning of the twentieth century was to find a room full of young children engaged in drawing pictures, building with blocks, looking at books, singing songs, and making clay creations. A teacher might be encouraging a child to examine the intricacy of a spider's web or a bird's nest, to gently plant a seed, or to investigate the work of ants. Wearing clean, if worn, clothes, these were not the children of the city's privileged class but of immigrant, working-class, and poor families. The children who entered the free kindergarten program were benefiting from Eliza Ann Cooper Blaker's unique combination of intellectual, creative, visionary, and practical educational leadership.

The growing midwestern city was fortunate to have attracted Blaker from her home in Philadelphia. An educator who had turned her passions to early childhood development, Blaker trained kindergarten teachers to engage the child's entire family in the educational well-being of the child. Her attention was on the physical and spiritual health of the entire family, with emphasis on attentive parenting,

ELIZA ANN COOPER BLAKER

as well as attention to cleanliness and practical homemaking. She was also interested in helping immigrant children develop an "American identity." Indianapolis mothers by the thousands heard Eliza state her theme, "The greatest work in the world is character making. You are in this work."

On March 15, 1854, in Philadelphia, Pennsylvania, Eliza Cooper came into the world as the first daughter of Jacob and Mary Jane Cooper. Jacob, of English Quaker ancestry, and Mary Jane, whose background was Pennsylvania Dutch, made their home in a city known for its antislavery activity.

When Eliza was seven years old, the country's Civil War began, and the city of Philadelphia prepared for the struggle of wartime life. Though most Quakers in the Northeast were opposed to slavery, the church, with its traditional peace stance, did not endorse military action to end it; Eliza's father, however, believed that nonviolent means could not end slavery and volunteered for Union military duty at the age of forty. Jacob Cooper was not an educated man, but he had a sharp mind and was an avid reader. He was known as a good conversationalist (although not a successful businessman) and instilled in his children a strong desire to learn. Complementing her husband's idealism, Mary Jane Cooper was practical, resourceful, and determined. Eliza inherited traits from both parents.

Like other soldiers who left behind family when they joined the army, Jacob relied on his wife to care for their children. Mary Jane Cooper asked her young daughter to take on household responsibilities. When her mother was hired by a Philadelphia shop to sew uniforms for soldiers, Eliza and her younger brother, John, spent time with their maternal grandmother in the German section of the city. From her they learned about prayer as well as cleanliness and thrift.

After months of worrying about Jacob, word reached the Cooper family that he was missing. Mary Jane went to look for him, leaving little John with relatives but taking ten-year-old Eliza with her. Their search led them to a hospital in Washington, D.C., where they found Jacob in critical condition. With his wife and daughter to care for him, his health gradually improved—despite the dismal conditions of the hospital. Eliza witnessed disturbing sights of physical trauma and suffering, but her mother helped her to bravely face these experiences, deepening Eliza's sense of sympathy for others.

Jacob eventually was well enough to return to Philadelphia, but he couldn't cope with a physically demanding job. The family opened a delicatessen and made their home in the rooms above the business. When a third child was born to the Coopers, Eliza had additional caretaking responsibilities, especially since Mary Jane had to take over the deli business when Jacob's health declined.

Eliza's father died when she was fifteen years old. Relatives urged her to find a job at one of the many cotton mills in the region, but Mary Jane was insistent that her daughter stay in school. She recognized Eliza's intellectual potential and wanted her to become a teacher. Eliza attended the Girls Normal School in Philadelphia, where she saw that her family was not alone in struggling to make ends meet. Having been taught by her grandmother to be thrifty, she walked 5 miles to and from school to save money. At one point, she was caring for her mother, who was ill and worn down from hard work, in addition to studying and going to classes. Three months before graduating, because of the family's severe financial problems, Eliza took a teaching job in the Philadelphia Public School System. Eliza then studied at night to finish her education and graduated, as valedictorian, with her Girls Normal School classmates.

Eliza continued to teach, helping fund her brother John's education at the University of Pennsylvania Medical School. He later graduated with honors and went on to become a successful physician in Albany, New York.

At the Centennial Exposition of 1876, Eliza Cooper encountered an exhibition that would change the course of her vocational life. Among the displays of "the finest achievements of the day in the fields of art, education and science," the young public school teacher watched a demonstration of a kindergarten that was structured around Friedrich Froebel's ideas for early childhood education. The kindergarten movement that had started in Germany (*kinder* meaning "child" and *garten* meaning "garden") was beginning to gain momentum in the United States. The program began as the result of Froebel's work. Froebel believed that young children needed to be provided with educational materials, activities, and experiences appropriate for each stage in their development. He proposed that educators needed to understand how children learn, and how to plan and facilitate a curriculum that would encourage children to explore the world around them. He also felt that an important part of education was to help children understand their connections to others and find their place in society.

Eliza, who was learning about urban social issues through her teaching in the Philadelphia Public School System, was captivated by Froebel's theories. She was convinced that establishing kindergartens could be an effective tool for social reform and soon enrolled in the Centennial Kindergarten Training School. What she learned would impact generations of Indiana children.

On September 15, 1880, Eliza married childhood friend Louis J. Blaker. Their simple Quaker wedding was held in the Cooper home, beginning a happy marriage that would last more than thirty years. Louis would be a stable, encouraging spouse, devoted to Eliza through what would become an intense and varied career in education. He provided judicious council when she, like her father, showed a certain level of impulsiveness.

After her marriage Eliza took a position as a teacher at Vine Street Kindergarten in Philadelphia. Then in 1882 she was invited to take charge of a kindergarten program for the prestigious Hadley Roberts Academy, a private school in Indianapolis. Louis was experiencing health problems at the time, and the couple thought a change of environment might help his condition. The Blakers moved to Indiana, and Eliza's mother and younger sister, Mary, came with them. Eliza and her mother remained close, and Mary followed in her sister's footsteps by completing her teacher training. Sadly, Mary died as a young woman. Eliza was devastated by her sister's death.

Near the end of the nineteenth century, the city of Indianapolis was experiencing a population boom, along with a boom's accompanying urban planning challenges. With more and more students, classrooms were swelling beyond capacity. New schools and teachers were needed. Additionally, the gap between the rich and poor was becoming wider—the mansions in upscale areas of town were like another world compared to crowded inner-city neighborhoods. Not unaware of the social problems, middle- and upper-middle-class women began organizing civic clubs.

Coming from the schools of urban Philadelphia, Eliza was attuned to the challenges facing children from poor families. Soon after she and her family settled in Indianapolis, members of the Indianapolis Free Kindergarten and Children's Aid Society approached her about starting a program. Given her passion for social reform, Eliza felt called to serve poor families and resigned from Hadley Roberts Academy. Women's social clubs helped her organize the kindergartens by providing money, supplies, and even clothing.

Eliza believed that everyone—regardless of class, gender, or race—should have access to quality education. She wanted no child to be turned away from school. She also initiated a new concept in early childhood education practices: emphasis on parental involvement in a child's education. Eliza believed that both teachers and parents should be concerned with character training for children.

Her philosophical approach emphasized the "harmonious growth of both the body and soul; the present well-being and happiness of the child, his preparation for home and school life and for future citizenship."

Froebel's theories served as a foundation for her work, but Eliza also developed her own methods and curriculum. While she believed it was critical to have a strong theoretical understanding of early childhood development, her primary focus remained on meeting the individual, day-to-day needs of the students in her classroom. She was also careful not to embrace every new instructional philosophy that came along.

Eliza was motivated to further share her educational knowledge and skills with her adopted community. She recognized a critical need to find and train kindergarten teachers and responded by beginning a teacher preparation program in her home. Known as the Kindergarten Training School, its first class of graduates—eight students—received their diplomas in 1883.

By the end of the first decade of Eliza's leadership, the free kindergarten programs were growing and gaining broader recognition. In 1892 Eliza was asked to serve as secretary-treasurer of the kindergarten division of the National Education Association (NEA). By the turn of the century, there were twenty-three free kindergartens in Indianapolis. Some of the programs were located in disadvantaged neighborhoods, supported by community parents who, while poor, wanted their children to receive a good education.

New worlds opened up to children who enrolled in the free kindergartens. They were introduced to arts, crafts, music, and nature, and given lessons about cleanliness and democratic decision making. Eliza also trained teachers to develop and organize playground activities.

In 1884 Eliza introduced the concept of mothers' clubs into the Free Kindergarten Society. She felt that the work of kindergarten

teachers would be more effective if mothers could provide supportive training at home. Teachers and members of the Free Kindergarten Society would make regular home visits in the kindergarten
districts, giving them the opportunity to share with parents the benefits of a kindergarten education and to understand the needs of
individual students.

The mothers' clubs in Indianapolis were among the first parent-
teacher organizations in the country. Mothers met to socialize and
attend classes that focused on childhood development and practical
aspects of parenting and homemaking.

Eliza used simple explanations when talking to the mothers
about the important role of parents in nurturing their children's
moral and spiritual lives. She stressed that spiritual aspects of parenting—love, sympathy, and understanding—were critical. She also
encouraged families to behave more like "republics" than "monar-
chies," which ran somewhat counter to the typical family structures
of the time.

In addition to her efforts to empower low-income women,
throughout Eliza's long career as an educator in Indianapolis, she
also paid attention to African-American communities and concerns.
Free Kindergartens were established in these neighborhoods and
clubs for African-American mothers were also initiated.

Special activities for older children were also created. On Sat-
urdays, classes were offered in "kitchen gardens" for young children.
Girls aged ten to seventeen received training in housekeeping,
including instruction on cooking, sewing, and making beds. Instruction for older students included food shopping, laundry, housekeeping, cooking, and dressmaking.

The Kindergarten Training School was renamed the Teachers
College of Indianapolis in 1905, unofficially called "The Blaker
Teachers College." The college continued to be governed under
the Free Kindergarten Society Board until 1913, during which

time Eliza served as both kindergarten superintendent and training school president.

In the early part of the twentieth century, it was difficult to recruit teachers into early childhood education training programs because of the limited financial incentives. The college began offering scholarships in an effort to attract young women to a two-year program that focused on childhood development theory and Froebel's educational philosophy and practice. As the college expanded, other courses such as literature, history, and psychology were added. The programs also emphasized the need for students to translate the theory they were learning into actual classroom situations. Students training to be teachers spent part of their days attending classes and the rest of their time practicing what they learned in kindergartens across the city.

The college did not charge tuition fees and so was funded entirely by private donations. Students were expected to help administrators, including Eliza, with fund-raising. There was no budget to build permanent facilities, so classes were held in a variety of locations. In 1903 the college opened a new building that included space for classrooms, a science lab, a gymnasium, and an auditorium.

By 1907 Indianapolis could boast that it had developed thirty-five free kindergartens throughout the city. Many of these schools were social centers as well as classrooms. Since the inception of the Free Kindergarten Society, 49,252 students had enrolled. More than 5,500 teachers had been trained to shepherd kindergarten programs.

Sadness entered Eliza's life when her mother died in 1908. Eliza had always admired her mother for her work ethic and for her insistence that her children be well educated—qualities that had inspired Eliza.

In 1913 Eliza became the president of the Teachers College when it was separated from the Free Kindergarten Society. Four years later, the college began awarding bachelor's degrees in pedagogy. Eliza also received a degree that year—an honorary doctorate from Hanover College of Indiana—acknowledging her work in establishing a nationally regarded training program for teachers.

While this stage of her professional life brought fulfillment, Eliza faced the personal challenge of surviving the grief over her husband's death. Louis Blaker died on April 28, 1913. To cope with the loss, she spent hours in Indianapolis's Crown Hill Cemetery beside her husband's grave.

In the last decade of her life, Eliza continued to devote herself to being an educator. At the age of seventy-two, having spent forty-four years devoted to early childhood education, Eliza Cooper Blaker suffered a heart attack and died quietly on December 4, 1926.

In the years immediately after her death, the Teachers College went into financial decline. An agreement with Butler University was reached in 1930 and the university paid off the debt of the Teachers College in exchange for property and administrative control. The joining of these two schools ensured that the contributions Eliza Blaker made to Indianapolis and to the field of early childhood education would not be forgotten.

JULIET V. HUMPHREYS STRAUSS

1863-1918

A Plain Country Woman

ONE SATURDAY MORNING, SEVERAL YEARS AGO, I got up with the feeling of being at the end of the rope . . . I was sick and tired and discouraged. I felt that it was too bad for me to be plough-ing around the kitchen at work when the sun was shining, and lots of people were out riding in parks, and sailing for Europe, and doing all of the beautiful things I was quite well fitted to enjoy but never got to do.

After I got the dishes washed, and the bread made up, and a cake baked, and the porches scrubbed, I remembered about two chickens I had put under a tub the night before to be dressed for Sunday. There was just about enough time to wring their necks and dress them and get them safely on ice before I started in to get dinner. But then I was seized with a violent attack of the dreadful "I don't want to's." . . . I didn't care for anything—I was at the end of the rope!

My mother used to have a way of taking down the Bible, opening at random and reading the seventh verse. She said it invariably gave you a clue to the solution of your difficulties. There was a big, old-fashioned dog-eared Testament on the table just within reach of my hand. I took it listlessly, opened it, ran my eye down to verse seven of the eleventh chapter of the Acts, which I happened upon, and read the words: "And I heard a voice saying unto me, Arise, Peter: slay and eat."

When I read the verse I broke out laughing. And when you are downhearted a laugh is the only thing that will cure you. I felt better instantly, got up, and went out and slew the fowls and got through the day in good shape.

—Excerpted from "The Woman Who Wears the Halo," a column by Juliet V. Humphreys Strauss originally published in 1908 and included in the collection of her work, *The Ideas of a Plain Country Woman*

Juliet V. Humphreys was born January 7, 1863, in Rockville, Indiana, an area which would be her lifelong home. She was the second of three daughters (a son died at the age of four) born to William and Susan Humphreys. William died when Juliet was only four years old. Finances became tight, and Juliet later remarked that she and her sisters made a "fine target for village gossips and for the slings and arrows of outrageous fortune as dealt out by more fortunate girls who [had] fathers and big brothers and money and 'social position.'"

But Juliet's childhood was not without happiness. One of her favorite pastimes was exploring the thick forests near her Parke County home, fostering in her a sense of independence as well as a love of Indiana's natural beauty. Her wanderings led her family to give her the nickname "Gypsy"—shortened to "Gyp." She also spent a lot of time with her mother who was devoted to raising "genteel" daughters and introducing them to literature and music. Though she was sharp minded, the young Juliet was not a serious scholar—she once said at a gathering of newspaper editors that she never studied a lesson in her life—but she did have "the close companionship of a cultured mother who had a vocation for teaching and who devoted her whole life to the care and education of her children."

Juliet excelled in one subject: writing. She often read aloud, using her talents to amuse her classmates (though other audiences were not always as appreciative). She would recall, "[P]reachers always fidgeted around and the nice ladies in their rustling black silk frocks coughed apologetically behind their folded handkerchiefs."

It was one of these literary works that caught the attention of *Rockville Tribune* editor John H. Beadle, who told Susan Humphreys that Juliet should be encouraged to expand her gift. Juliet's mother had to be convinced that it would be acceptable for her daughter "to do anything of a public nature," but finally agreed that Juliet could write for the *Tribune* to perhaps pick up shorthand.

The family nickname that stayed with Juliet through young womanhood was the inspiration for the *nom de plume,* "La Gitani," under which she wrote her first newspaper article, a lively description of a Rockville social event. The story launched her writing career as well as her relationship with newspaperman Isaac R. Strouse, who kept her authorship of the piece anonymous by typesetting the copy when no one else was in the office. The two also found a mutual love of literature, and they were soon a serious couple.

The Humphreys family had concerns about Juliet's intended spouse. When she told her uncle that she intended to marry a man whose lifework was in newspapers, Juliet said her uncle "chewed on a piece of straw for a moment" before telling his niece, "Jule, don't you know that being an editor is the orneriest business in the world?"

These concerns, however, did not deter the relationship, and the couple married on December 20, 1880, when Juliet was nearing her eighteenth birthday. Neither had earned a high school diploma—Strouse had left school at age sixteen—but Juliet passed

JULIET V. HUMPHREYS STRAUSS

exams to become a teacher, even if she would only teach for a short time.

If he didn't realize it before their wedding, Isaac Strouse soon discovered that his wife had an independent streak when it came time to sign her married name. Strouse's father had altered the spelling of the family name from the Germanic "Strauss" to "Strouse." Juliet, however, insisted on using the traditional German spelling of her husband's name throughout her life, though Isaac continued to use the Americanized version.

After Isaac became partners with Beadle in running the *Rockville Tribune* in 1882, Juliet began writing for the newspaper once again. One day when Isaac was the only one in the office to run the press, a man requested that a relative's obituary be written and published in that week's edition. Isaac told him that to add the story when the edition was nearly put to bed might be impossible. The man insisted and offered to pay for this service, though there was usually no charge for printing obituaries. Isaac took the money and had it changed into a five dollar gold piece, then went home to offer it to his wife if she could get the obituary written in time. She took the challenge and earned the gold.

In June 1883 Juliet gave birth to the first of two daughters, Marcia Frances; Sarah Katherine was born in January 1887. In 1889 Isaac became the owner and editor of the *Rockville Tribune*. Four years later, in February of 1893, Juliet Strauss began writing a weekly column for the paper, "Squibs and Sayings." She soon discovered, however, that "news was scarce and society items few and far between." She later said, "I had to dig out what I wrote from my head." Her life at home as a mother and wife was also a significant source of writing material.

Isaac contributed little to the parenting of his two daughters, spending much of his time at the newspaper. Juliet later reflected that there were two types of men: a domestic man who will "go to church with his wife, and set the hens, and run the clothes through the wringer, and read aloud from the farm paper while [his wife] fashions garments for the little ones from the worn-out raiment of their elders"—and "the other kind." According to Juliet, her husband was "the other kind." Isaac "was a sportsman, a man of the streets and town, a man's man in every sense of the word—and I was a mother, a child in years, but I had to make a world for my children, a castle to build—and how was I to build it unless I learned to make bricks without straw." Keeping a household going was hard and, for her, often lonely work, which likely contributed to her statement later in life that husbands were "all right I guess, if you have to go somewhere and all the other women have them."

Though the newspaper was a family business of sorts, Juliet was also finding a deepening sense of vocational calling as she developed her writing style. In a town as small as Rockville, she would not find many mentors, but the community did provide quick feedback when one of her columns met with disapproval. One incident that hurt Juliet was when the *Tribune*'s rival newspaper printed what she described as "a long, sarcastic, venomous criticism of me and my work." What kept her writing were the readers who found her work to be a source of delight. "You would be surprised to know," she said, "how well a kind or helpful word . . . is remembered all a lifetime—and too, how, though you may forgive them, the unkind word or act remains—a hurt that never quite heals."

She also found encouragement from outside Rockville circles, including from other Hoosier writers like John Clark Ridpath, James Whitcomb Riley, and George S. Cottman. When Juliet asked Cottman to critique her writing, he praised her ability to capture the "picturesque character" of the Rockville community and life in Indiana at the end of the nineteenth century. He also told Juliet that she needed to improve her ability to tell a story and to work at developing her unique voice.

In a response to Cottman's letter, Juliet wrote that she indeed had a passion for portraying old times. She also told Cottman about the tension she felt trying to balance housework and parenting responsibilities with her writing. She lamented that she had little time for reading and also confessed a dislike for the work for which she had become best known—newspaper writing. In March of 1897 she informed Cottman that she could not take part in the annual meeting of the Western Association of Writers. "I have so very many cares and so much hard work to do that I can find little time for writing," she wrote. Nevertheless, she was on her way to becoming one of the day's most widely read American female writers.

The year 1903 brought another set of contradictions to Juliet's life: personal grief and public success. Her mother died in January, and later in the year—as she struggled to find time to write amid the never-ending succession of family responsibilities—her efforts as a columnist attracted the attention of *Indianapolis News* editor Charles R. Williams. An essay Juliet had written about the month of April prompted him to hire Strauss to write a weekly installment of "common-sense, down-to-earth observations on life" for Indiana readers. Her "Country Contributor" column first appeared in the November 21, 1903, edition of the *News*.

In her writings as much as in her own life, Juliet continued to emphasize the importance of a woman finding her place at home, and the dignity and worth of homemaking over the fashionable and elegant lives lived by society ladies. "Being a plain home woman is one of the greatest successes of life," she argued, "if to plainness you add kindness, tolerance, and interest, real interest, in simple things." She challenged those who believed that a country woman led a less meaningful life than a woman from the city, writing that, "It is the woman who has walked across the fields on a wild winter night to help a sister woman in her hour of trial, the woman who has dressed the newborn baby and composed the limbs of the dead, learned the rude surgery of the farm, harnessed horses, milked cows, carried young lambs into the kitchen to save them from perishing in the rough March weather—it is she who has seen life."

Juliet became well known throughout the state and became a frequent public speaker. Two years later, it was a national publication that came calling. Edward Bok, the editor of the *Ladies' Home Journal*—the most widely read women's magazine at the beginning of the twentieth century—had noticed one of Juliet's "Country Contributor" columns in the *Indianapolis News*. He wrote, "It struck me as well done. I watched it for some time. Then I took pains to find out who wrote it."

Thematically, the *Ladies' Home Journal* focused on a woman's identity as centered in the home, in how she saw to the needs of her husband and children. Even though Juliet was spending more and more time away from her domestic duties to write and give public lectures, she supported this philosophy wholeheartedly. She prided herself "on plain living and high thinking" and affirmed the traditional role of women as family caretakers. But she was also experiencing the dilemma of a woman caught between her career and her responsibilities to home and family. She grew frustrated when she didn't have enough time to spend on her writing. She wrote articles for the *Ladies' Home Journal* that reflected on her conflicted feelings about the time-consuming tasks of cooking, cleaning, and other domestic chores, and the joy she found in them. Women across the country identified with this struggle for balance and came to think of Juliet as a mentor and a friend. Juliet's journal columns were edited and collected in *The Ideas of a Plain Country Woman* (1908).

Her economic and social status changed as Juliet and her husband rose from struggling newspaper owners to influential community members. But the couple didn't find a natural place in Indianapolis social circles, nor did they completely fit in with other rural families.

Juliet's ideal remained the woman who appreciated culture but understood the importance of focusing on the health of her family and neighbors. This perspective was increasingly challenged as women joined the labor force in large numbers, became involved in social reforms, and found alternatives to work at home.

Juliet Strauss, born in 1863, would have much in common with many women who were born fifty or even one hundred years later, especially in terms of struggling to balance her care for home and family with the demands of her professional life and goals. She lived in an age when conventional gender roles were slowly changing in a number of areas of society, but she still appreciated what she felt was the noble role of woman as the keeper of hearth and home. She didn't enter social clubs or join her contemporaries in demanding voting rights for women. She was particularly critical of what she called the "smart" ideal of womanhood—the perfectly groomed and well-mannered lady. "I say she is tiresome, that her 'taste' is questionable, that her influence on society is unwholesome," she wrote. "I hope my women friends will begin a reform with resolutions to be less like somebody else and more like themselves, to do as they wish to do, not as some other woman sets the pace."

Juliet may have struggled to reconcile her desire for literary success with an equally strong yearning to be a devoted wife and mother, but her household eventually settled into a regular routine: Juliet would write her columns for the *Indianapolis News* and *Ladies' Home Journal* on Mondays and Tuesdays and would spend time in the next few days writing or dictating replies to the dozens of letters she received each week from her readers. Bessie Skelton, who served as Juliet's secretary for six years, said that her employer was adamant about responding to each piece of mail. Toward the end of the week, Juliet prepared her "Squibs and Sayings" column for her hometown newspaper.

"Very seldom did she hesitate about subject matter. The words seemed to flow from the end of her pen," Bessie Skelton recalled. "She often said to ambitious and inquiring readers, 'The only way to write is to write.' That was all she could tell them—that was her experience."

But Juliet's work schedule did not prevent her from being available to her daughters. "Her first and last thought was always for the children—they must have a good, wholesome time," Bessie stated.

Juliet's daughter, Marcia F. Strouse Ott, who followed in her mother's footsteps to become a columnist herself (for the *Rockville Republican*), described her role model as "the most passionate mother I have ever seen." Ott recalled that her mother "bruised her heart and hands alike . . . to make the way smooth for her children." Juliet could not heal her family's every hurt, however, and in 1912, her younger daughter, Sarah, died at the age of twenty-five.

Eventually, and perhaps in a high point, Juliet applied her passions and professional connections to saving a cherished piece of ground from exploitation. In 1916 the Hoosier Veneer Company of Indianapolis prepared to pay $30,200 at auction for a vast acreage of virgin forest near her hometown of Rockville known as Turkey Run. Upon learning of the imminent sale of this land, then called Bloomingdale Glens, Juliet teamed with other conservationists to stop the sale. With Indiana conservationist Richard Lieber and two others appointed to a Turkey Run Commission by Indiana Governor Samuel Ralston, she lobbied both in her newspaper column and from her regional public-speaking platforms. Others on the commission sought legislative means to stop the sale of what Lieber called "a paradise of rocky gorges, glens, bathing beaches and waterfalls."

Lieber had earlier approached the governor about establishing a state park system to celebrate and memorialize the centennial of Indiana's statehood. The centennial itself was being organized by the Indiana Historical Commission (IHC). In January 1916 the IHC approved a motion to establish the state park movement—an act that paved the way to the protection of Turkey Run as well as other wildlife areas across the state. But then came the auction, and the sale of the land. All their efforts to that point had proved to be for nothing.

Indianapolis News reporter William Herschell met Juliet Strauss on the Sugar Creek trail following the sale of the beloved land to timber interests. "I am sick of soul," she told him. "Who would have dreamed that a few men's dollars could step in and destroy all this, the most beautiful spot in all Indiana, one that all the money in the world could not restore once it is gone?"

Herschell said that while the fifty-three-year-old nationally known writer was distressed, she was determined to keep up the fight to save Turkey Run. Juliet continued to speak and write about the need to preserve this beautiful forest. Six months later, the state was able to purchase the property for $40,200.

Her accomplishment in conservation and preservation came only two years before the end of her life. Four years after her passing in 1918, she was honored for her significant contribution to the state with a sculpture commissioned by the Woman's Press Club of Indiana. The sculpture, titled *Subjugation,* was created by Myra R. Richards as a tribute to Strauss and her body of work. According to the Woman's Press Club, it expressed the concept of "subjugation of the material to the spiritual."

Juliet's strong feelings about preserving the natural beauty of Turkey Run for future generations were perhaps more straightforward than those she had on the many topics she addressed in her three decades as a columnist and public speaker. On many other themes—marriage, the women's suffrage movement, women in the workforce, the responsibilities of the homemaker—Juliet expressed independent opinions that seemed almost at odds with the "plain home" image she painted for her readers.

Juliet was regularly ill in the last years of her life, but she always rallied to write her columns. For the *News,* she supplied pieces that could be printed in case she couldn't produce an article in a given week. Just one week before her death on May 22, 1918, Bessie Skelton called the newspaper to request that one of the "emergency" columns—on file in the newsroom in case Juliet couldn't produce a fresh piece—be returned to Strauss for revision. The fifty-five-year-old Strauss made the changes she desired and resent it to her editor. A few days later, she died.

Her last column, "In Defense of Exaggeration," appeared in the *Indianapolis News* on May 25, 1918. The *News* honored Juliet Strauss, stating that her columns offered "a very sound and helpful philosophy. One can read in them a love of simplicity and genuineness, an earnest and honest faith, a hatred of sham and pretense, and a belief in the home and family as the great educators."

While the style and content of her columns and essays may seem flowery and old-fashioned to modern readers, Juliet's own writing perhaps best reflects her life. She was proud that she had "never followed anybody's lead. I lived my own life. If I wished to ride a horse, or play a game of cards, or go wading in the creek with the children, I always did it. I never strained my eyesight or racked my nerves to arrive at small perfections. I avoided rivalries and emulations. In short, I lived."

GENE STRATTON PORTER

1863-1924

Naturalist and Author

THE FILMY LIGHT OF SUMMER DAWN trickled through dense forest canopy and into Gene Stratton Porter's bedroom, illuminating a miracle unfurling before her eyes. The chrysalis she had carefully attached to her pillow the night before was stirring. She had woken to a moment of transformation—the rebirth of a winged creature emerging from its fragile cocoon.

Though she had watched many creatures develop and thrive, Gene was fascinated anew by the beauty and design of the natural world. She had filled her life with moments like these. From the time of her childhood on her family's farm in northern Indiana, she had cultivated a passion and commitment for observing, photographing, and writing about the earth and its creatures.

Born in Wabash County on August 17, 1863, Geneva Stratton was the final child born to Mark and Mary Stratton. Mark, a farmer and Methodist minister, loved literature, while both of the Strattons were interested in the natural world. By the time Geneva was born, the family farm included flower gardens and orchards, and the large Stratton family—with a dozen children—was living comfortably.

GENE STRATTON PORTER

Like the rest of the family, Geneva had farm chores. She was responsible for taking care of the chickens, but she also had plenty of freedom to explore the nearby woods and streams, searching for Indian artifacts, catching butterflies and moths, and finding feathers. She also followed her brother and father around the farm as they worked. Not a typical girl of the day, Geneva spent more time outdoors than indoors.

Mary Stratton—described by her daughter as eminently "capable"—was known for her green thumb. She showed Geneva how to nurture slips and cuttings into climbing plants, trees, and shrubs. Geneva recalled later that her father had told her that plants and animals were a gift from God. Mark Stratton had also taught her how to gently approach wild creatures, once tying a handkerchief over young Geneva's nose and mouth so she could peek in a bird's nest without disturbing its residents with her breath.

Even as a girl, Geneva was inspired by the natural world. In an early attempt at writing (for which she would eventually become known worldwide), she wrote an "Ode to the Moon" on the inside of a schoolbook, though she would later recall that she didn't know then what an ode really was. In a book she would later write, *What I Have Done with Birds,* she wrote, "In one season, when under ten years of age, I located sixty nests, and I dropped food into the open beaks in every one of them. . . . Playing with the birds was my idea of fun. . . . It did not occur to me that I was learning anything that would be of use in after years."

The life of the prosperous Stratton family was visited by sadness in 1872 when Geneva's sister Mary Ann died in an accident. And then later in the year her beloved brother Laddie drowned in the Wabash River. Geneva was eight years old. She would later fictionalize this event, but in the resulting book, *Laddie,* the story of the brother and sister would end happily.

Seeking better medical care for Mary Stratton, the family relocated in 1874 to Wabash, Indiana. She had never regained full health after surviving a case of typhoid less than a decade before. She died in 1875.

Geneva continued to defy the conventions expected of typical young women of her era. She attended school until 1883, leaving without regrets before receiving her diploma. She believed that what she learned through her study of the natural world was the most beneficial education for her. While more proper and delicate young ladies of upper-middle-class backgrounds spent time on activities like sewing or music, Geneva preferred to hike through the woods and study birds. Considered strange by her peers, Geneva felt like an outsider in social situations.

But in 1884 while visiting Sylvan Lake in Rome City, a popular northern Indiana resort, Geneva's uniqueness was an attraction for Charles Darwin Porter, an industrious druggist from Geneva, Indiana, vacationing in the area. The two corresponded throughout an eighteen-month courtship. Geneva shared with Charles her concerns about confining marriages as well as her appreciation for traditional family roles. They were wed and moved to Decatur, Indiana.

In 1887 the newlywed Porters welcomed a daughter, Jeannette, and in 1888 the young family moved to Charles's former home-town of Geneva, Indiana. Charles Porter started a bank and drilled oil wells on his property. Perhaps to avoid confusion with the name of her new village, Geneva Stratton Porter began calling herself "Gene." She began exploring the surrounding area, a landscape covered with forest and marshland called "Limberlost." (Years before, a local man named "Limber Jim" had disappeared in the boggy area.)

In 1895 Gene and Charles moved into a new home of their own design, a fourteen-room cedar dwelling they called Limberlost Cabin. Gene spent time keeping the home tidy and caring for her daughter. She studied violin, took embroidery and china-painting classes, and joined a literary club.

Gene also spent considerable time in nature study in the marshes, jotting down observations and sometimes painting. She soon had enough material to send her first submission to *Recreation* magazine, but did not submit any illustrations. In her book *Homing with the Birds,* Gene would recall, "The editors who had accepted my work began to send me drawings of mounted birds, articulated with wire, stuffed with excelsior, and posed by men . . . [but] those pictures repelled me. I was horrified."

In response to this, Gene decided to learn about photography and take pictures to accompany her writing. Jeannette bought her mother her first camera—a four-by-five Vive model for which she paid ten dollars—as a Christmas present in 1895. Gene mixed her own chemicals to develop her film, create plates, and tone and wash her prints. The family bathroom became her darkroom and she washed her prints in the sink, using her own dishes from the kitchen to contain the chemical baths she needed.

In her first attempt to take and develop a photograph, she chose her pet parrot as her subject. While the print was "sadly undertimed and overdeveloped" and "contained almost every defect of a beginner's work," Gene saw that the image was "a perfectly natural, correct reproduction of a living bird. I had found my medium! I could illustrate what I wrote myself!" She later sold some family jewelry to buy a larger camera and began the serious work of photographing wildlife.

Gene expressed pride in her role as a wife and mother but, as she wrote in *Homing with the Birds,* she also yearned for an outlet "for the tumult in my being." Reflecting on her mother's struggle to balance family and career, Jeannette Porter Meehan wrote in *Lady of the Limberlost* (1928) that "the fever to write had raged within Mother until it became a compelling influence and dominated her whole life, her home, her entertainments, her amusements, and her work. After I was old enough to go to school, Mother spent many secret hours with her pen."

Since her neighbors were not aware that she had been submitting her writing for publication, Gene rented a post office box in case her work was rejected. A first story, "Laddie, the Princess, and the Pie," was published in *Metropolitan* magazine in 1901, and a clerk in her husband's drugstore saw the piece and complimented her on it.

She then sent a story to *Century* magazine editor Richard W. Gilder, who liked the piece and encouraged her to expand it into a novel. The story was about finding and burying a cardinal that had died from a gunshot. The imagined biography of the bird, set in Limberlost, became the book *The Song of the Cardinal,* which she also illustrated. While the book wasn't an immediate success, over time it became very popular and was translated into seven languages. But Gene had her detractors; there were those who questioned the scientific accuracy of her observations about natural history.

Throughout her publishing career, literary critics did not take her fiction very seriously, rejecting the "sugary" version of life she offered. The scientific community also largely disregarded her wildlife studies. Many were skeptical of her attempt to cultivate interest in nature among a mass readership by weaving in idealized, sentimentalized human characters. Though her characters met challenges, Gene avoided writing about the dark side of human nature or life's harsher realities. One modern critic noted that Gene's writing "continually sketched an America without tears. In her fictional worlds bad people were punished and honorable people were rewarded; goodness always prevailed over evil."

But Gene's stories proved popular with readers, who liked reading about birds in a way they could understand. Gene received letters from people who said that they had started or rediscovered an interest in nature through her books. She stated, "I care very little for the magazine or newspaper critics who proclaim that there is no such thing as a moral man, and that my pictures of life are sentimental and idealized. They are! And I glory in them! They are straight, living pictures from the lives of men and women of morals, honour, and loving kindness."

The inspiration for Gene's second book, *Freckles,* published in 1904, was a black vulture's nest in a hollow log. Charles had helped her find the carrion eater after Gene saw one of its feathers fall while the bird was in flight. She photographed the nest for several months, capturing the egg-to-hatchling transformation despite being surrounded by mosquitoes, gnats, snakes, and the smell of swamp muck. In addition to descriptions of nature, *Freckles* included the story of a breezy romance. Again, the book was not an immediate best seller. Eventually, however, more than a million copies of the book were sold in the United States, and readers in Great Britain purchased half a million. The book's 1909 sequel was even more popular: *A Girl of the Limberlost* is the story of Eleanora, a friend of Freckles, who finds moths in the swamps that she sells in a quest to save money for her education. Both *Freckles* and *A Girl of the Limberlost*—today perhaps her most well-known title—each sold two million copies.

During this productive period, Gene took daily field trips to the swamp, carrying both her camera and a gun just in case. The Limberlost swamp, she would write in *What I Have Done with Birds* (1907), "yielded me the only complete series of Vulture studies ever made, dozens of studies of other birds, material for a novel, more natural history stuff than could be put into several big volumes, many rare specimens and much priceless experience in swamp work."

Called "Bird Woman" by her Indiana neighbors and readers, Gene continued to seek kinship with the birds she encountered. "In spirit I say to the birds, 'Trust me and I will do by you as I would be done by . . . Trust me, and go on with your daily life. For what small disturbance is unavoidable among you, forgive me, and through it I shall try to win thousands to love and shield you.'"

Gene published one best-selling book after another in the early part of the twentieth century, including *The Harvester* (1911), about a woodsman, and *Laddie* (1913), a fictionalized version of her relationship with her older brother and her girlhood adventures in the forest. For many years, her fiction and nonfiction sold at a rate of 1,700 copies a day in the United States. She also had thousands of fans worldwide.

About the cabin in which she grew up, Gene's daughter, Jeannette, wrote:

> Almost any place in our house you might find a glass turned down over a little patch of moth eggs on a rug to protect them . . . a wounded bird, which was being doctored, perched almost anywhere . . . several different size boxes containing baby caterpillars just hatched, feeding on the particular kind of leaves that they ate . . . cocoons pinned almost anywhere, and newly emerged moths and butterflies flying through the house and feeding on the flowers in the conservatory.

Surrounded by God's creation, Gene's spiritual life was nourished. About God, she wrote:

> He may be the good in each one of us. He may be the invisible Hand that evolves and governs the Universe. He may be a great personality sitting on a far throne, ruling the world inexorably. Whatever He is, He is truly the spirit of worship that is born in the heart of every living creature when it begins to palpitate as a separate entity.

As her studies took her deeper into the heart of the natural world, Gene decided to concentrate on nearby swamps, woods, and meadows as the best laboratory for observing wildlife. But despite her efforts to share the beauty of the natural world with others, Gene saw further destruction of the precious places she hoped to preserve.

The Porters made their home in Geneva, Indiana, until 1913, when the Limberlost area that Gene Stratton Porter had made famous came to barely resemble the landscape of her youth, owing to the encroachment of oil and logging interests. In *Moths of the Limberlost* (1912)—the research for which required close observation of cocoons, leading her to pin fragile specimens to her pillow—Gene wrote:

> Soon commerce attacked the swamp and began its usual process of devastation. Canadian lumbermen came seeking tall straight timber for ship masts and tough heavy trees for beams. Grand Rapids [Lumber Company] followed and stripped the forest of hardwood for fine furniture . . . Afterward hoop and stave men and local mills took the best of the softwood. Then a ditch, in reality a canal, was dredged across the north end through my best territory, and that carried the water to the Wabash River until oil men could enter the swamp.

The Porters sought a place where Gene could continue to study nature. They found it in Wildflower Woods at Sylvan Lake near Rome City, Indiana, where Gene and Charles had first met. Gene called it Limberlost North. She also bought 120 acres at the south end of Sylvan Lake, where winding roadways led through forest and valleys.

In an article for *The American Magazine,* published in August 1919, Gene wrote:

> Because my house did not contain a suitable workshop, because my location had been devastated by lumbermen, farmers, and oilmen until it was impossible to find natural history subjects to illustrate my nature books, and because by that time I had earned sufficient money to do as I wished, I decided to change my location. I moved to a lake shore in northern Indiana, typical Limberlost country.

With the money she earned from her book sales, Gene had the opportunity to create perfect spaces for living and working. Shaded by beech, tulip, and oak trees, she described the two-story, fourteen-room home as "a big log cabin, having a secluded library, printing-room, dark-room, and every photographic convenience I could think of for my work, shut away from the remainder of the household."

Gene also wanted to create a safe place for flora and fauna to thrive. She hired Frank N. Wallace, a tree surgeon, to help her develop a healthy, wooded sanctuary on her property. A crew of workers cared for damaged and sick trees and helped Gene transplant woodland flowers into six one-acre beds, each of which was devoted to showcasing a single color.

The Porters made the new Limberlost into a woodland utopia, eventually incorporating around 17,000 plants, vines, flowers, trees, and shrubs. Gene transplanted many of these, even adding rare seeds and plants sent to her by fans from around the world, including everything from indigenous orchids to arrowhead lilies, rosemary to ferns.

Around this time, Gene published two more books, *A Daughter of the Land* (1918), a story of farm life, and *Homing with the Birds* (1919), which she completed after returning from a month-long stay at a health clinic in New York where the fifty-four-year-old had gone to rest and distance herself from distressing news of World War I.

In 1919 Gene surprised her neighbors and readers alike by selling her beloved cabin and leaving her Hoosier home for a completely different habitat: Los Angeles. Though she had lived in the lush greenery of woodland Indiana her entire life, Gene found a new love for the ocean, deserts, and canyons of California.

Seventy-year-old Charles Porter remained in Indiana to tend to his business, visiting his wife during the winter. Jeannette and her two daughters moved to California with Gene.

Though Gene was a private person who had long found companionship among winged creatures and leafy neighbors, she began socializing more than she had in the Midwest. She wrote to friends,

"I have lain aside boots and breeches and put on crepe and beaded chiffon and a French bonnet with roses and a veil; and I stand up and speak my little piece with the best of them." She also wrote that she most enjoyed the sunshine of the West Coast, but also liked meeting:

> actors, poets, authors, painters, sculptors from all over the world. . . . Fine folk these artistic and creative people be! Some of them are self-seeking and selfish and pushing, as is the manner of humanity, but most of them are world-experienced, educated in adversity, a real treat.

Gene didn't give up everything she knew, however. She continued writing, publishing editorials for *McCalls* magazine, advising middle-class American women on everything from gardening to growing old gracefully. She also wrote poetry and penned the novels *Her Father's Daughter* (1921) and *The White Flag* (1923). She continued to promote wildlife conservation, both in writing and through public speaking.

Long before it was fashionable, Gene Stratton Porter issued warnings about preserving the world's natural resources. She advocated for the protection of birds—including ducks, passenger pigeons, wild turkeys, and owls—and forests and swamps. Like another powerful figure in the early twentieth century, President Theodore Roosevelt, Gene realized that America's land, forests, wildlife, clean water, and air were being compromised. Wrote novelist Grant Overton, "Each, beyond all possible question, has influenced human lives. Neither was oppressed by the enormous responsibility attached to such a role."

Eager to reach even wider audiences with her message, Gene sought out Hollywood filmmakers who encouraged her to take her books to the silver screen. She created her own motion picture company, Gene Stratton Porter, Inc., to make films that were true to her novels, including *The Girl of the Limberlost*. While her films were not blockbusters, they were considered successful.

Gene found clear differences between the stories she wanted to tell and the movies being produced by the popular film industry. Advocating for less sex and violence in Hollywood pictures, she tried to find ways to engage parents, educators, and churches in pressuring the producers to tell more wholesome stories. "Every dollar of money" that went into her films, she said, "I earned myself, most of it in the fields and woods and in the swamps. . . . It is the extent to which I am willing to go in order to prove that our young people are being shown the wrong kind of pictures."

Wanting to leave a legacy for her home state, Gene sought to sell Wildflower Woods to the State of Indiana. She had plans to build a cabin in California like the one she had left behind in Sylvan Lake and to create a natural wildflower and bird sanctuary. The sixty-one-year-old purchased five acres of land on Catalina Island.

Though Gene had completed many ambitious projects throughout her life, this was one she did not fulfill. On December 6, 1924, Gene was only blocks from her home when a streetcar struck the limousine in which she was riding. She suffered serious injuries from being thrown from her vehicle and was unconscious when she arrived at the hospital. She died two hours later.

Gene was mourned by fans from around the world and honored by a number of national and international entities. Her Indiana homes and Wildflower Woods have been made into state historic sites, where visitors can see the results of her conservation work. A forest of 10,000 white pines was dedicated to her in Adirondack Forest Preserve. Her Limberlost cabin has been designated as an Indiana Historical Site, open for visitors in Geneva, Indiana, near the former Limberlost Swamp (now known as Loblolly Marsh, with 400 acres restored to watershed conditions). Gene is remembered as a writer who keenly observed the outdoor world, who had sold ten million books by the time of her death, and who taught many people from all walks of life to appreciate what buzzed and bloomed around them.

ALBION FELLOWS BACON

1865-1933

Housing Reformer

IF ALBION FELLOWS BACON HAD, at some level, believed that her visit to "Old Saint Mary's" in Evansville would be a social call, the dismal tenement apartment she found upon arriving disabused her of the notion. Little in her life had prepared her for seeing this level of poverty. There was garbage in the hallways and a single water cistern to serve the entire riverside tenement. Dirty children stared at her, dark eyed and suspicious.

Having arranged to visit some of these less fortunate residents, Albion was now meeting families in their one-room dwellings. She asked them why the building was not kept clean and in good repair and learned that there was no money. While the city's diverse manufacturers offered employment, these were low-skill, low-pay jobs—and the homes of the workers reflected this gloomy reality.

Albion had only recently started to pay attention to the less-desirable facets of life by reading about poverty-related issues and following local politics. Her comfortable, middle-class life had been occupied with taking care of her husband and children, housekeeping, growing flowers, listening to music, reading, visiting friends, and attending social gatherings. Albion had not paid attention to the places in her hometown where life wasn't so pleasant. By her own description, she had lived a "sheltered life."

But something was stirring in her—a spiritual yearning to link her faith with her social concerns, a sense that she had the skills to address the injustices she was seeing. Having given up on her dream of college years before, yet possessing the intelligence and passion for education, Albion began seeking ways to aid, educate, and advocate for the poor. Her visit to the tenement would be only the first of hundreds of such visits across the state, each renewing her resolve to make Indiana homes safer and healthier.

On April 8, 1865, Mary (Erskine) Fellows gave birth to her third daughter. Widowed several weeks before, she named the newborn after her late husband, the Reverend Albion Fellows, a Methodist minister who had succumbed to pneumonia at age thirty-eight.

Mary Fellows never remarried, raising her daughters alone. The family of females relocated to McCutchanville, Indiana, where life revolved around the girls' schooling, nearby cousins, seasonal farm activities, and the Methodist church. A strict mother, Mary taught her daughters to value literature and supplied them with many books. The girls also took an interest in titles like *Pilgrim's Progress* from their late father's collection of books.

Albion and her sister Annie, who was two years older, were close companions throughout their lives. Beginning in childhood, they shared similar interests. Both enjoyed art and had a passion for poetry, committing many verses to memory in order to recite their favorite odes and epics to one another while doing their chores around the house. When Albion was fourteen and Annie sixteen, the sisters submitted their writing to *Gems of Poetry*. Both were successful in publishing a piece. Albion wrote about nature, spiritual themes and the supernatural.

In 1881 the Fellows women moved back to Evansville, where Albion completed high school in two years and graduated as class salutatorian, delivering a commencement address about the impact of the works of Elizabeth "Mother" Goose. Her speech was in some ways typically Victorian, with flowery language and lofty ideals. Albion clearly admired the woman who had done "what greater geniuses could not do . . . [made] the heart of childhood merry with your simpl[e] melodies, which still ring a sweet accompaniment to the memory of our early joys." What Albion didn't understand then was that an ideal childhood was not the reality for many young Hoosiers, nor did she know that her destiny would include a strong interest in addressing their needs.

Albion's own youth was swiftly coming to an end, and she was looking forward to moving beyond the world she knew. She wanted to go on to college to study art, but family finances were too tight. Instead she went to work as a court stenographer, learning about business and legal records. In the male-dominated worlds of business and politics she was often the only woman in the room. Her confidence grew as she became accustomed to going "without fright into public buildings, to keep my own counsel, and to avoid feminine flutterings."

Her work wasn't as intellectually stimulating as her dreams of college, but Albion was earning needed money. She also had a beau, Hilary E. Bacon, a banker and dry goods merchant, to whom she became engaged in 1888. Her sister Annie also gained a fiancé that year, and the two decided to travel abroad together before they married. They set sail for Europe, visiting Ireland, Scotland, England, Germany, Switzerland, and France. In London, the sisters ordered their wedding gowns. They enjoyed a double wedding on October 11, 1888, after which Albion gave up her job in order to devote herself to the care of her home and the comfort of her husband.

In September of 1889 the Bacons welcomed their first daughter, naming her Margaret Gibson. A second daughter, Albion Mary,

ALBION FELLOWS BACON

was born in January of 1892. After this second birth, Albion became ill with persistent fatigue and depression and was diagnosed with nervous prostration (neurasthenia). While she was devoted to her young family and by all external appearances was living a pleasant life, Albion continued to wish for ways to engage her intellect and perhaps express some independence. Her world seemed small.

Albion recovered slowly. In 1896 she and Hilary moved their family to a new house, and Albion and her sister again joined forces to coauthor a volume of poetry, *Songs Ysame,* which was published in 1897. Albion also became more involved in community social circles, joining the Woman's Foreign Missionary Society and the Ladies and Pastors Christian Union.

But she wasn't interested in local social welfare and civic-reform efforts. In fact, she actively sought to "exclude every ugly or blighting thing" from her life, ever ignoring modern fiction and newspapers. Since she was a little girl, when she had been told in church that exposing herself to the darker side of humanity would leave a stain on her soul, Albion had avoided troublesome stories, choosing poetry instead. "If, after carefully choosing a book, the turning of a page disclosed an unexpected 'problem' or ugly suggestion, I threw it from me in disgust, as I would a fine peach with a worm in it," Albion later reflected. "As to newspapers, I read the poetry first, skimmed the headlines, and skipped the politics, turning under the crimes and accidents."

But in small ways, Albion began to look beyond her cocoon of privilege. First, she began to work with civic leaders after visiting her children's school and finding the playground to be inadequate. Later, after an outbreak of scarlet fever in her neighborhood, Albion noticed that some children—not as clean and well dressed as her daughters and their friends—were coming to school with red spots and sores. Out of concern, she joined the sanitation committee of the Civic Improvement Association, though she didn't yet understand the challenges for poor families or the links between economics, education, and health.

If she could take part in civic work, Albion felt, she should also do some church work. She tried helping a ladies' church committee with its Easter bazaar, but it made her feel "exhausted and puzzled." She would later reflect:

> I can't think of Christ as being on a committee, or as giving us that kind of work to do. I felt I needed a spiritual tonic, and I thought some such work would build me up, but it didn't seem to suit my case. . . . [T]hen, with a sudden curiosity, I seized my Bible, and began turning over its pages to see what Christ had said about work being spiritual "meat." How much stress He laid on "serving"! And how strictly he enjoined upon us the care of the poor!

Around that time she met Caroline Rein, the general secretary of Associated Charities of Evansville, who arranged for her to visit the "Old Saint Mary's" area—a riverside tenement not served by the city's sewer and water lines. Albion couldn't get the images of poverty out of her mind. She later wrote:

> I looked down into the backyard, littered with broken crockery, cinders and tin cans, and strewn with garbage, over which hovered swarms of flies. . . . In one place a slimy stream oozed away to the alley. . . . A sickening odour of old vaults, sour suds and decayed garbage rose to our nostrils.

She also recorded a conversation she'd had with a tenant whose circumstances were dire. The woman had said with tears in her eyes,

> We must get some decent place to move up to. It's awful here. We've always lived in the country, and here we are right on the

street, where we hear people passing by, and there are so many that go by here cursing and swearing. The men come in drunk at all hours of the night. There's no lock on the door. We push the bed against it, but we're too frightened to sleep. And then, these hot nights, that dreadful smell comes up from the yard and we have to shut the window. My God, such a place!

Albion also met a mother whose young son had contracted tuberculosis. The sick boy had nowhere else to lie but on a thin, moldy mattress on the floor. Albion asked whether the woman had gone to the landlord for help, and the woman replied that she had, but that he had refused to do anything. Furthermore, there was no law by which he could be forced to.

Struggling to respond to what she saw, Albion implemented Rein's vision of organizing a group to visit the poor. As a "Friendly Visitor" she soon began helping to sort out family difficulties and to negotiate disagreements between tenants and landlords. She also addressed everyday challenges such as parenting issues and maintaining cleanliness. A Visiting Nurse's Circle was formed, and Albion often accompanied nurses to the homes of poor families to care for children and adults suffering from tuberculosis, pneumonia, typhoid, dysentery, and other illnesses. She also formed a group of men's visitors, generally business people.

Albion tried to maintain a balance between her home life and her benevolent work by volunteering her time during the hours when her children were in school. She had to curtail her activities when she became pregnant with twins, giving birth in 1901 to Hilary Jr. and Joy. In 1903 Albion entered social welfare work again. She founded and led the Evansville Flower Mission, introducing her children to charitable endeavors by having them sort and deliver flowers, thus forming friendships with less fortunate families.

Albion was also concerned about the circumstances of Evansville's "working girls"—young women who labored at low-paying factory jobs. Albion joined a committee to investigate these less-than-ideal workplaces and was appalled at the working conditions she found. The Working Girls' Association was formed to provide young women with nourishing yet affordable food, safe housing, and a place to socialize, with the goal of keeping them from losing their self-respect or, worse, turning to prostitution.

Social welfare initiatives continued to expand in Evansville. But despite hard work, Albion felt that the efforts "to alleviate the wretchedness of the poor" did not result in permanent positive change. In *Beauty for Ashes,* a book published in 1914, she wrote:

> The stream of misery flowed on, unchecked, and seemed to be growing larger. We had been doing almost nothing to prevent the evils whose ravages cost so much to repair . . . I began to notice how the threads of the social problems, the civic problems, and even the business problems of a city are all tangled up with the housing problem, and to realize that *housing reform is fundamental.*

In 1908 Albion decided to draw on what she had learned while working in the courts to work toward a solution to substandard housing. She initiated a yearlong public lobbying effort directed at the health committees of both the State of Indiana House and Senate, asking for regulations and oversight of tenement health and safety issues. The bill she put forward would set standards for the living conditions in multiple family dwellings. It was passed by the Indiana legislature in 1909 and applied to tenements and apartment houses in Evansville and Indianapolis. After spending significant time in the state capital, making important connections with legislators and other influential men and women, Albion returned home in the summer, ready to establish an office for a building inspector.

Albion didn't have long to relish the victory. In the fall of 1909, the Bacons' eldest daughter died at the young age of twenty, from what is believed to be the result of a congenital heart problem. After a difficult year Albion emerged from a grieving period and picked up where she had left off. In October 1910 Albion delivered a speech entitled "Women, the Legislature, and the Homes of Indiana," at the Indiana Federation of Clubs' (IFC) annual convention.

Though she didn't go so far as to move her family into a run-down neighborhood, Albion made sure she didn't separate herself from the realities of the poor. "Before I started off on a tour," she wrote in *Beauty for Ashes,* "I went again to the homes of the poor, to burn within my mind a more vivid image of their wretchedness, to get the figures of their enormous rentals, and to rouse afresh the anger that blazed within me, that I might kindle it in others."

In 1911 Albion was instrumental in the formation of the Indiana Housing Association—the first such organization at the state level in the country. The association stated that its goal was "to protect and foster the Homes of Indiana by encouraging right housing conditions, and by helping to eliminate those unfit, unsafe, and unsanitary conditions which are a menace to morals, health, safety, and comfort."

Leaving home once again to lobby for the improvement of shelter for others, Albion traveled throughout the state in 1912 as a representative of the IFC and the Indiana Housing Association, giving speeches in thirteen Indiana cities and towns, conducting tours and investigations in nine, and speaking to several State Board of Health entities. Her message was that the State of Indiana should establish housing standards laws. For all of her efforts, Albion was nicknamed "Indiana's housekeeper."

Other states were beginning to take notice of Indiana's new laws. In December 1912 Albion was invited to speak about the nation's housing problems at the second annual conference of the National Housing Association in Philadelphia. In her speech she stressed the need for sanitation and fresh air and advocated for healthy living standards.

The lobbying Albion began in 1909 was, by 1913, a well-organized, politically savvy campaign, focused on bringing a statewide housing legislation bill to the Indiana General Assembly for the third time. After lengthy debates, and to Albion's credit, a housing law was passed in 1913—a significant step, though it would impact only incorporated cities, not rural areas or suburbs.

Albion's autobiographical work, *Beauty for Ashes,* focused on housing reform, particularly her 1909, 1911, and 1913 lobbying efforts of Indiana's General Assembly. She also wrote the book to persuade readers of the importance of Christian service and to inspire women in particular to contribute to positive changes in their communities. Albion wanted women to be inspired by the civic work of women's groups. Years after the publication of *Beauty for Ashes,* Albion found out that it was being used as a text at universities across the country, including Union Theological Seminary. This brought her an immense sense of satisfaction, since she had long been disappointed at not having attended college herself. "I feel that I have a few things to pass on, especially, and most of all, a great and unusual faith in God and in immortal life," she would later reflect in an unpublished memoir.

Albion continued her writing. With a typewriter set up first in her bedroom and later in a remodeled third-floor room that she called her "treetop typery," Albion devoted countless hours to her work. In 1928 she published a tract titled *Finding God*—a memoir about faith that she hoped would inspire those struggling to find a spiritual path. Later, in *The Path of God,* she wrote, "I believe that the Spirit touches all of us in ways of which we may not be aware. What else are those strong convictions of duty that swing us about at times like a strong hand?" The *Charm String,* released in 1929 by L.C. Page & Company, was her only published work for children.

But Albion's social welfare work wasn't nearly done. In 1917 she supported the passage of a law that would allow for unsafe or unsanitary houses to be officially condemned—the so-called deathtrap law. As the active leader of the executive committee of the Indiana Child Welfare Association and with the State Commission on Child Welfare, Albion lobbied for the passage of child labor and school attendance laws. She also worked to have child welfare committees appointed in every county.

With so much accomplished in these important laws, a friend reportedly asked Albion what social issue she might tackle next—perhaps suffrage? Albion's answer was typically forthright: "No, housing reform. Housing till I die. I have made only a good beginning." But she would see work in areas related to children and youth as very much a part of her home-focused reform advocacy.

In April 1918 Albion began participating in a wartime program initiated by the Federal Children's Bureau in Washington, D.C., called the "Children's Year" campaign. The first goal of the program was to weigh and measure all preschool children to roughly determine the health of the children. Albion led efforts in Indiana to collect this data on information cards—despite some challenges in getting chairwomen in every county to cooperate. This huge project was tiring for Albion, and resources were lacking. She nevertheless also took up another initiative of the Children's Year campaign, which was to develop back-to-school/stay-in-school and recreational activities for young people, as an attempt to reduce the wartime rise in juvenile delinquency. Meanwhile, she also organized a state conference on child welfare, including a session to address the topic "What the State Is Doing to Protect Her Children." She later addressed a child welfare session at the annual meeting of the State Conference of Charities and Correction, in her talk entitled "The War Comes Home to Indiana."

In 1919 Albion joined the Indiana Commission on Child Welfare and Social Insurance. The committee recommended the creation of a juvenile commission, a child-labor law, and a school attendance law. Legislation was created to bring Indiana's requirements for school attendance and employment of youth closer to the standards proposed by the Federal Children's Bureau. With few exceptions, children between the ages of seven and sixteen were required to attend school, most paid work was prohibited to those under fourteen years, the hours that children could work were limited, and employment in hazardous jobs was prohibited.

State legislators did not create a juvenile commission, but they did act to create the position of a state juvenile probation officer. Albion was elected president of a newly created Advisory Juvenile Committee to oversee the work of that office. Albion continued to pay attention to these issues and in 1921 addressed the Indiana General Assembly in Indianapolis about improving Indiana's system of juvenile justice.

Scaling back her public work in the 1920s, Albion began to take fewer speaking engagements and traveled less. She remained active with the state's Advisory Juvenile Committee. She also continued her work with the Visiting Nurse's Circle, which was later incorporated into the Public Health Nursing Association.

During the time that Albion served on the Evansville Zoning Commission, the city committee planned street design, recreation facilities, and railroad and harbor development. She also became a member of the Committee on Standards and Objectives—an initiative of President Hoover to address housing issues—to which she proposed:

A home should be a shelter and a protection, a retreat from the world with privacy and quiet; it should be safe from danger to life and limb, from fire, from intrusion, and from moral hazards; it should not be overcrowded; it should have outlook; it should have dryness, absence of dampness and foul odors; it should be kept in repair; and it should have convenience, comfort, and beauty.

Albion's passion for housing reform was tied to her advocacy work to address health issues like tuberculosis. She became involved in tuberculosis prevention efforts and supported the establishment of Boehne Camp, which later became the well-known sanitarium Boehne Hospital, and a summer camp outside of Evansville for children who were at risk for contracting the disease. The Vanderburgh County Tuberculosis Association voted Albion as its president in 1932.

The next year, on December 10, 1933, "Indiana's housekeeper" died of arteriosclerotic heart disease and chronic nephritis. She was sixty-eight. According to her daughter Joy, "Mother just burned herself out." Local newspapers all referred to Albion Fellows Bacon as Evansville's "best known and most loved woman."

MADAM C. J. WALKER

1867–1919

Millionaire Entrepreneur

INDIANAPOLIS NEWSPAPERS REPORTED ON an impressive story in 1911:
Sarah Breedlove Walker, the daughter of former slaves, the woman
who had built up the Madam C. J. Walker Manufacturing Company
of Indiana from a kitchen-based business into a thriving hair-
product industry, was pledging a $1,000 gift to the city's YMCA
building fund for African-American boys and men. While not a
native of Indianapolis, Sarah, or "Madam" as she'd christened herself, was welcomed there.

Sarah's husband, Charles J. Walker, and the company's lawyer
Freeman Ransom had convinced her that a donation to the YMCA
would bring a splash of positive publicity for Walker Manufacturing, which had recently filed its articles of incorporation. A savvy
marketer who put her own picture in newspaper ads for Walker hair
products, Madam agreed. It was one of her many gifts to the city.

Months earlier, on September 12, 1911, the three members of
the company's board of directors—Madam C. J. Walker, her daughter,
Lelia McWilliams Robinson, and her husband, Charles J. Walker—

had signed the papers that offered capital stock in the company at $10,000 (1,000 shares at $10 per share). The company, described in legal documents as manufacturing and selling "a hair-growing, beautifying and scalp disease-curing preparation" was worth then around $25,000. This kind of success was unheard of by a "colored" businesswoman, even one who was quickly becoming an icon of sophistication and success.

Philanthropy was an extension of Madam's deep faith and her wish to help others who had also grown up poor and wanted a better life. In a visit to Dr. Booker T. Washington's Tuskegee Normal and Industrial Institute in January of 1912, Madam made a promise to herself that she would give money to educational causes. She lamented that, at age forty-four, it was harder to learn new things than it had been when she was young. But she had been born into poverty and had struggled to raise her daughter on the meager wages of a washerwoman, with no time or money for advanced schooling.

What set Madam apart was that she had found the will to change her destiny. In the words she used to inspire others, "I got my start by giving myself a start." Through her intelligence, creativity, and perseverance, Madam C. J. Walker made life better for herself, her daughter, and thousands of others. By creating a marketing phenomenon with her beauty products, she became the first African-American woman millionaire. With her wealth came elevated social status and the opportunity to speak out against racial oppression and lynching, as well as a means for helping others.

Sarah Breedlove was born on December 23, 1867, in Delta, Louisiana, to Minerva and Owen Breedlove—former slaves who had become sharecroppers on the Burney cotton plantation. Arriving just a few days before the fifth anniversary of the Emancipation Proclamation, Sarah was the first among her siblings to be born free. Of course, southern sharecroppers didn't live completely free lives,

MADAM C. J. WALKER

tied as they were to the whims of the weather, crop prices, and white landowners. The family worked hard to scratch out a living in the highly segregated community.

Adding to the difficult circumstances, Minerva Breedlove died when Sarah was young. Owen soon remarried, but died two years later, leaving Sarah an orphan at age seven. Later in life, she would say that she "had little or no opportunity when I started out."

Sarah went to live with her older sister Louvenia in Vicksburg, Mississippi. She was expected to work and had little time to spend on schooling. But she found a way to do both, taking some lessons at the African Methodist Episcopal Church and doing laundry work.

Louvenia was married to a man named Jesse Powell. Powell insisted that Sarah contribute to the family income; he also became physically and emotionally abusive and squashed Sarah's budding hopes of obtaining further education. Her teachers had been encouraging, but Sarah's home life was too oppressive. When she was fourteen years old, Sarah met Moses McWilliams. Rather than stay in the Powell household, she decided to marry him. While she talked about her church wedding later in life, no marriage certificate has ever been found and none may have been filed. It is possible that a marriage bond at the time would have been too costly for the couple.

Several years into married life, on June 6, 1885, Sarah gave birth to a baby girl. The couple named her A'Lelia, and Sarah became immediately devoted to her. As a young mother, Sarah continued to launder the clothes of middle- and upper-class clients. Moses found various jobs, including fieldwork. They were eventually able to move into a house, and two consecutive years of good crops brought better wages. But then Moses died unexpectedly in an undocumented incident in 1887 or 1888.

Sarah did not want to go back to live with her sister and

brother-in-law and decided to leave Mississippi. In 1889 she took Lelia and headed for St. Louis, where her brothers—Alexander, James, and Solomon—owned a barbershop near the well-known St. Paul African Methodist Episcopal (AME) Church.

In St. Louis, Sarah again took up work as a laundress. It was unenviable and dangerous work, involving irritating lye soap, wooden washtubs, iron pots of boiling water, and heavy, red-hot flatirons. Throughout the laundering process, if Sarah caused a snag, lost a button, or scorched a shirt, she had to compensate her employer out of her paltry weekly wage of between $4.00 and $12.00.

In St. Louis Sarah attended St. Paul African Methodist Episcopal Church—the second oldest black Protestant church in the city and the oldest AME congregation west of the Mississippi River. The congregation was socially and economically diverse, made up of working-class people like Sarah as well as doctors, teachers, lawyers, and social leaders. Sarah was aware of their differences. She regretted that she had not been able to continue her education and was embarrassed by her appearance. Perhaps because of her laundry work, the time she had spent with toxic soap and hot water, she had an unhealthy, itchy scalp. It didn't respond to popular treatments or the home remedies suggested by friends.

In 1894 Sarah married a man named John Davis—a decision she would come to regret. A drinker, John was moody and turned violent toward Sarah. In later years, she tried to erase all record of the relationship and never talked about it.

Sarah had high hopes for Lelia. When her daughter wasn't accepted into Sumner High School, Sarah was determined to save her money and send Lelia to Knox College, one of the few institutions in the Midwest to offer high school and college programs to African-Americans, specifically to the descendents of former slaves. Lelia entered Knox at age seventeen and was placed in the seventh grade. Sarah took charge of her own education as well and began attending night classes, hoping to improve her success as a small business owner with a laundry service.

On a path to self-improvement, Sarah separated from John. She was feeling more confident and soon met Charles Joseph Walker, called C. J., a well-liked bachelor who often traveled to Indianapolis for his job as a sales agent for a newspaper in Denver, Colorado. She remained concerned about her appearance and was particularly self-conscious about her hair. Tucked under a head wrap—a style practical for field hands and domestic workers—her thin and unhealthy hair wasn't conspicuous, but women in the city maintained more fashionable coifs that required long locks. For working women, given the typically infrequent washings, scalp diseases, and harsh hair treatments of the day, a very healthy head of hair was relatively uncommon. Another photo taken around this time reveals that Sarah, dressed in a prim, high-necked blouse decorated with a brooch, has a poof of dry, frizzy bangs. Frustrated with her damaged hair "breaking off and falling out," Sarah tried many products "without result" and eventually became nearly bald.

Distressed, Sarah prayed about her situation—and, as she would later testify, God answered. "One night I had a dream," she said, "and in that dream a big black man appeared to me and told me what to mix up for my hair. Some of the remedy was from Africa, but I sent for it, mixed it, put it on my scalp and in a few weeks my hair was coming in faster than it had ever fallen out." She may also have learned about some of the healthful properties of other ingredients from a doctor.

She tried the formula on Lelia's hair and then with her neighbors and began operating a small salon in her home amid her other work. In trying to heal her own dreadfully painful scalp and hair, Sarah was changing her life.

In 1903 Sarah became one of the earliest sales agents of hair products developed by African-American entrepreneur Annie Minerva Turnbo. In 1905 Sarah moved to Denver, Colorado, to sell Turnbo's Wonderful Hair Grower. Sarah moved in with her brother Alex's widow and daughters. Lelia was still in school so Sarah arrived without her beloved daughter and with only $1.50 in her pocket. Ever the hard worker, Sarah found work as cook. She soon moved into a place of her own.

Known as a ladies' man, C. J. courted Sarah—and gave her advice about selling her hair treatments. Part of his advice involved newspaper ads. The two were married on January 4, 1906; Sarah was thirty-eight years old.

While it isn't known whether she used Turnbo's products or whether it was her own mixture that ultimately saved her scalp and hair, Sarah soon distanced herself from Turnbo and began selling her own scalp conditioner and healing formula. She used her married name, but with an elegant twist: "Madam Walker's Wonderful Hair Grower." She thought the title of "Madam" lent a certain air of sophistication to her products.

Sarah, now known as Madam, would say that she was a "hair culturalist," and that her products were designed to heal scalp disease through a process of frequent shampooing, massage, and application of ointment containing petroleum and medicinal sulfur.

What were the "wonderful" ingredients in her products? Though the exact formula was a secret, a thick petroleum served as an oil base, beeswax acted as a stabilizer, copper sulfate and precipitated sulfur were used as sanitizers and healers, carbolic acid served as a disinfectant, and violet extract covered the smell of the sulfur. The Madam Walker system may also have used coconut oil, a commodity that would have been hard to procure in St. Louis but may have come from the west coast of Africa. The idea that ingredients for the balm were rare and obtained with difficulty added to the mystique of the product.

Soon the entire family was involved in selling Madam Walker products. Lelia moved to Denver to help manage the business, and Madam and C. J. traveled among U.S. African-American communities to promote the product and build a mail-order business. Madam spent a year and a half selling the products throughout the South before moving to Pittsburgh, Pennsylvania, where she discovered it would be easier to make shipping arrangements.

In Pittsburgh Madam began to train a sales force to help her sell the hair products. In 1909 she personally trained fifty-one agents—women and girls—in Wilberforce, Ohio. The saleswomen shared testimonials from customers for whom the treatments had worked, including Mrs. W. A. Snead of Columbus, Ohio, who wrote to say, "I have not the knowledge or words to express my gratitude for what you have done for me. My hair is about seven inches in the front and six in the back, and as thick as a woven rug."

The Madam Walker hair product business continued to be family managed. While Madam made extensive trips to expand her market, Lelia was put in charge of keeping the salespersons stocked with supplies that were stored in her home. During this time, Lelia married John Robinson (although, strangely, Madam did not attend her daughter's wedding). Lelia soon took responsibility for managing the Pittsburgh-based office while Madam traveled to conduct training sessions and make sales. Madam also began to look for another base of operations.

In 1909 Madam created "Lelia College" in Pittsburgh, which trained agents to sell the Madam Walker products. By 1910 the college had trained around 1,000 salespersons. "Walker Agents" became familiar throughout the United States and in the Caribbean. These salespersons were instructed in a successful marketing strategy that is still replicated today: Agents would visit friends, neighbors, and clients in their homes or host them in small salons, then demonstrate the products and provide testimonials about the effectiveness of the hair growth system. A Walker Agent was to wear a crisp, professional uniform consisting of a white shirtwaist tucked into a long, black skirt.

In addition to the hair grower that had started it all, the Madam Walker line expanded to include pomade and sixteen other beauty treatments. Because she was no longer embarrassed by her hair, products carried a label that bore the likeness of Madam C. J. Walker, who was well on her way to becoming one of the most widely known African-American women in the country. She kept up a constant travel schedule in order to give "instructional tours" and to personally encourage sales agents.

The Madam Walker products were advertised nationally, mostly in black newspapers and magazines. The *African Methodist Episcopal Church Review* would reflect, at the time of her death years later, that Madam "owed her success not alone to the merit of her commodity. It was far more due to her ability as an organizer, her faith, as well as talent, in advertising."

While her business was growing by leaps and bounds, Madam's marriage was on a downward slope. She wanted her relationship with C. J. to be solid, but was suspicious about his behavior. Rumors were spreading that her husband was not being faithful to her, and that C. J. was misusing company monies. Madam hoped that a move would provide an opportunity for them to have a fresh start in a new community.

On February 10, 1910, Madam and C. J. Walker arrived in Indianapolis, Indiana, and found a friendly, firmly rooted African-American community. With a significant number of successful, black-owned businesses in the city and excellent connectedness to other parts of the country thanks to eight railroads, Madam felt she could make Indianapolis her national headquarters.

Fulfilling her dream to have a home, a factory, a laboratory, and a salon, Madam purchased a two-story house in Indianapolis for $10,000. Not yet a millionaire, she continued to work hard to pay for and furnish the home. In addition to serving customers in a salon on the property and assembling the ingredients for her hair products, she also ran a boardinghouse and cooked for her tenants. And she still did her own washing.

During this time, she met Charlotte Hawkins Brown, an African-American teacher who became a friend and tutor, and who helped with the training of sales agents and beauty shop operators. Madam also employed African-American lawyer Freeman Ransom, a former railway porter, who became the company's business manager.

With the help of a trusted staff, Madam continued her tireless travel schedule. In the summer of 1910, she went to African-American conventions and fraternal and religious meetings from Indiana to New York. She impressed investors and customers, who could tell how committed she was to growing her company. It was a successful year, at the end of which Madam Walker had earned nearly $11,000—around $200,000 in today's currency.

Madam had made her Indianapolis residence an elegant home and had become an important businessperson in the city, often visited by prominent citizens and visiting dignitaries. Her factory and business office employed around three dozen people. She had transformed herself into one of the respected, well-off churchgoers she had observed so closely in St. Louis.

But not all news was good in 1910. Lelia's husband deserted her less than a year after their wedding, and Madam convinced her daughter to move to Indianapolis. Meanwhile, Madam's own marriage continued to be troubled. Though she loved C. J., she was embarrassed by his affairs with other women and began making plans to separate from him.

Though Madam was a member of Indianapolis's affluent African-American community, she didn't disconnect herself from those who were less fortunate. She helped poor neighbors with rent or groceries and gave coins to children who ran errands for her home-based salon. She generously gave out turkeys and food baskets during the holidays. A religious woman, Madam believed that God was good to her because she had made a point to give to others. She used her public-speaking platforms to encourage African-American women and girls to take charge of their lives by obtaining an education and otherwise bettering themselves.

Her sales agents also benefited from her encouragement to make a better life for themselves—through having a small business (running a salon and selling her products), gaining self-esteem, and taking pride in their appearance and presentation. One agent wrote to her in 1913, "You opened up a trade for hundreds of colored women to make an honest and profitable living where they make as much in one week as a month's salary would bring from any other position that a colored woman can secure."

When Madam's divorce from C. J. Walker was finalized, Lelia convinced her mother to buy a home in Harlem and to establish a New York City business base. Once again, Madam bought a house that would accommodate living space, a beauty salon, and place for a school to train salon operators. She began dividing her time between Indianapolis and Harlem and left most of the day-to-day business management to Freeman Ransom, her attorney as well as her general manager, and Alice Kelly, the forewoman of the Walker factory.

Madam C. J. Walker was ahead of her time in building a business through strategic advertising, "word of mouth" marketing, and personal sales. In 1916 she organized her sales force into "Walker Clubs" in preparation for a convention the following year and offered cash prizes to the most philanthropic clubs. At the 1917 annual Walker convention, agents shared treatment and styling techniques and talked about their experiences; then Madam gave awards to the clubs that had given the most to their local communities.

In addition to encouraging her agents to do benevolent work to benefit African-American communities, Madam was deliberate about giving to black charities and organizations. When the National Association of Colored Women initiated efforts to secure the home of Frederick Douglass to preserve it and turn it into a museum, Madam contributed the largest single donation to the successful cause. She made significant contributions to the National Association for the Advancement of Colored People (NAACP) and funded homes for the elderly in St. Louis and Indianapolis. She especially remembered the needy in Indianapolis during the Christmas season and continued support of the YMCA. Impressed with the mission and programs of the Tuskegee Institute, she decided to underwrite scholarships for students. She also contributed to Palmer Memorial Institute, a private secondary school for African-Americans in Sedalia, North Carolina, founded by her close friend Charlotte Hawkins Brown.

Sarah "Madam C. J." Breedlove Walker died on May 25, 1919, at age fifty-one after a lifetime of hard work. Though her doctors had cautioned her about her busy work schedule, she had remained an active businesswoman despite health problems. The cause of her death was kidney failure and complications of hypertension. She was buried in Woodlawn Cemetery in Bronx, New York. An Associated Press article described her as the wealthiest black woman in the country, "if not the entire world . . . credited with having amassed a fortune of more than one-million dollars through the sale of a 'hair restorer.'" A prominent African-American publication praised her, observing, "Her largest legacy is the inspiring example she has left to ambitious souls to undertake the achievement of large affairs." *New York Age* honored her for her philanthropic work and for helping "the race on its upward stride." Others were complimentary about her pioneering efforts in hair care, including improving the personal hygiene of thousands and thousands of women. The Walker Manufacturing building that had served as the center of Madam's business in Indianapolis was refurbished in 1927 and became the Madam Walker Theatre Center. It was placed on the National Register of Historic Places in 1980. Through her model of success, her philanthropy, and her efforts to advance the causes of African-Americans across the country, Madam and her hair products transformed an untold number of lives.

MARIE GOTH

1887-1975

Portrait Artist

THE ESTEEMED HOOSIER POET James Whitcomb Riley sat fidgeting before artist Marie Goth, watching as she carefully applied color to her brushes and studied the way the summer light settled across his wide nose and cheekbones. Then she carefully set brush to canvas.

"I was just barely learning how to paint. I had learned how to load my palette and the colors I should use," Marie recalled. "Mr. Riley had had a stroke, and his right side was affected." She also noted that he "wasn't as gruff as anticipated but he became impatient easily." With relatively little time each day to work with Riley, it would take Marie several months to complete the portrait.

In Marie Goth's career, she would paint the portraits of prominent individuals from many walks of life including university presidents and movie stars. She would come to be recognized as one of Brown County's most notable residents as well as one of Indiana's finest portrait artists.

Marie Goth was born in Indianapolis in 1887, to Jessie and Charles A. Goth. She grew up surrounded by a loving, close-knit

MARIE GOTH

group of extended relatives. She and her father enjoyed a close relationship through Marie's childhood. She once told a story from her childhood about her father ripping out an illustration of the fairy tale "Beauty and the Beast," because the picture had frightened little Marie.

Marie's first years in school were unexpectedly difficult for a bright young girl, but the adults around her soon realized that Marie needed eyeglasses. Her vision eventually cleared, however, and she quickly made up for lost time. The gift of clear sight would reward her later in life.

Another gift was music. Marie's father was a bass violinist with the Indianapolis Symphony Orchestra. "When I was very young he used to take me to rehearsals, where I would sit all evening listening to music and enjoy wearing my little white angora fur collar and muff." Her mother was a fine contralto, and the whole family shared music, both with instruments and voices. Marie and her younger sister, Genevieve, grew into skilled pianists, and Marie had a strong soprano voice.

By the time Marie finished grade school, an interest in visual art had bloomed. As she considered her options as to where to attend high school, she said she:

> found it necessary to decide which of the two high schools I wished to attend . . . [T]his was not a difficult decision to make because I knew the head of the art department at Manual Training High School. He was an artist who had studied several years in the art schools of Paris. He also painted beautiful pictures and was my father's cousin.

The cousin, Otto Stark, was one of the Hoosier Group painters—an esteemed school of Midwest artists first identified by a writer in the 1890s. The school also included John Ottis Adams,

William Forsyth, Richard Buckner Gruelle, and Theodore Clement Steele.

"Now because of this connection I did not expect to receive any special attention, but was hopeful of being in one of his classes," Marie noted. Stark's influence was very much evident throughout the art department. In addition, Marie would recall valuing her exposure to larger traditions of art. "Beautiful pieces of sculpture, reproductions of the work of masters such as Michelangelo and others, were visible and impressed me greatly." Marie loved her drawing classes at Manual Training High School and excelled at the techniques she was learning. At the age of sixteen she won first prize in a citywide design contest. Later, she took classes at Indianapolis's John Herron Art Institute. In 1909 she won a scholarship to study in New York City at the Art Students League. Her initial goal was to become an illustrator, but she gradually turned her attention to painting.

When she moved to New York, Marie lived near the Hudson River at the Three Arts Club—a boardinghouse lodging eighty-five young women who were studying art, music, and dance in the city. On Sunday afternoons the music students often gave voice or piano concerts, and the club also held dances and other social events. Among her acquaintances, Marie met a music student who gave her singing lessons in exchange for a painting.

Marie continued to win scholarships at the New York Art Students League. In 1912 she wrote a modest letter home to tell her family about her accomplishment: "It is as little as I can do to make you proud of me when you have deprived yourselves in so many ways in order to help me make the most of myself. I thank you for allowing me this opportunity and as I have said before, whatever success I have is due all to you."

Marie was only three years older than her sister Genevieve, and the two shared a close relationship over the course of their lives.

When they were young, much of their days were spent playing together; at night, they were tucked into the same bed. When Marie went to New York, Genevieve sent Marie part of her week's wages to help pay Marie's art school tuition and living expenses.

During the third winter that Marie spent studying at the Art Students League, the Lyons Toothpaste Company paid her $100 to paint the portrait of a contest winner. She later recalled that she impulsively spent the paycheck "on some dresses, a raincoat, and a writing case."

Living in New York City was expensive, especially with art supplies to purchase. Marie tried to supplement her income with a job that involved brushing luminous paint onto the faces of wristwatches and the dials of weaponry manufactured for use in World War I. She could earn $80 to $100 a month for finishing 250 pieces per day, but she only completed a week's worth of work before quitting out of boredom with the tedious job. Though she may have needed the money, it was a fortunate decision; much later, Marie learned that some of the girls she had worked with had become ill from ingesting the radium in the luminous paint, having twirled the bristles between their lips in order to create a finer brush tip.

At the Art Students League, Marie took lessons with Frank Vincent DuMond, then esteemed as one of the best artists of his day. It didn't take long for Marie to decide that she wanted to make portrait painting her life's work. She would study with DuMond for the next ten years.

Marie was engrossed by her studies in New York, but also missed her family back in Indiana. Her friends and relatives wrote her letters that kept her up to date with news from home and encouraged her in her studies. Her father once turned the family's living room into an art gallery bare of furniture but filled with Marie's paintings and drawings. Friends and relatives bought a few of the sketches at the "show."

At the Art Students League, Marie met another aspiring artist, V. J. Giuseppe Cariani. They enjoyed a budding romance, but Cariani, a native of Italy, felt strongly about participating in the American military and enlisted in 1917. When he returned from fighting in World War I, he was "dispirited" and retreated to his immigrant family's home in Springfield, Massachusetts.

In 1919 Marie returned home to Indianapolis, even though she knew she would miss the sights and sounds of the Hudson River. But she soon adjusted to the landscapes of the Midwest and set up an art studio in her parents' house.

Marie and Cariani—called "Cari"—exchanged regular letters. Marie did not want to give up on the relationship and went to her father for advice. Charles suggested that he offer Cariani a stone-carving job at Crown Monument Company, the family-owned business Charles shared with his brother. Cariani accepted the job and moved to Indiana, staying for a time at the Goth home.

Three years after Marie returned to Indiana, her sister Genevieve purchased a cabin in Brown County, south of Indianapolis. The cottage was located at the end of State Road 135 off a muddy, rutted cow path—but its vistas provided plenty of inspiration for Marie, who took up flowers as a subject in addition to her portraits. Their father made several pieces of furniture for the small building, and the two sisters took donated items from their relatives and family treasures from the basement to furnish the rest. Oil lamps provided their light, and the mattresses were made of straw.

"Each piece is a souvenir," Marie wrote of her furniture, "and although no one else would have any of it, I do enjoy the lot of it." The cabin would remain largely the same for the next fifty years.

Cari lived in the cabin during the week. Genevieve and Marie resided in Indianapolis and traveled to the country cabin on weekends. Then Marie's mother fell ill and could no longer climb the stairs to her second-floor bedroom in the family home, so Marie had to vacate her studio so her mother could rest on the main floor. Marie needed studio space to continue her painting, so she moved to the cabin in Brown County. Cariani soon moved out so as not to ruin Marie's reputation, building a studio of his own nearby.

A friend of the couple would later state that Cari:

> did all the gardening, [and] I heard that he did all the cooking in her home. The way I understand it he lived in his studio, which had no kitchen, and she in her home. They ate their meals together in her cabin. He was a very gentle and refined man, and they were of a vintage that they were discreet. But you couldn't help but see her love for him when they were together. I don't think they could have been closer if they had been married.

Another person who knew the artists agreed, saying, "Marie and Cari were lovers. Oh yes, it was accepted, well known, and some thought they were even married. But they weren't married." Cariani was a lifelong, devout Catholic and adhered to the principle of not marrying outside of his faith; Marie's religious background was Christian Scientist.

In moving to Brown County, Marie met a number of artists and other community residents who became close friends, including the Thomas and Ruth Morton family. Marie painted both of the Mortons, their daughter Susan, and Thomas Morton's prizewinning stallion, Majestic Ensign.

Marie received her first commissions in professional portrait painting in the early 1920s. To paint the portrait of James Whitcomb Riley was an honor, but despite this high-profile assignment, it would take several more years for Marie to gain broader recognition. She continued to look for interesting faces to capture with paint and canvas. She would reflect years later in an interview for the Brown County *Democrat,* "For it took twenty years of long-hour days of experimenting just to control my oils, so they wouldn't be too runny, nor too tacky. This cannot be taught. You must keep working at it until you get it absolutely right."

Marie entered a portrait she had painted of Charles W. Dahlgreen in the 1926 Hoosier Salon, winning first-place recognition for "Best Portrait in Oil." In 1931 her painting, *Florence*, received the Julia A. Shaw Memorial Prize in the annual exhibition of the National Academy of Design in New York; the award came with a $300 prize. Marie wrote later that she:

> was surprised and delighted. The people who gave the prize invited me to visit them. So I did and saw my portrait of Florence hanging in the gallery of the National Academy of Design. And I was pleased. It was indeed a highlight in my artistic career.

The people who visited Marie's log house, coming from near and far to have her paint their portraits, were her "sitters"—subjects who posed while she carefully worked to capture their appearance and character. Marie was known to take up to a week to capture the hands of her subject to her satisfaction.

> Despite the demands and difficulties involved, I've enjoyed every portrait I did, and still do. Most sitters comment on my complete silence at work, but once I get into a painting, I'm completely absorbed during each challenging session . . . until I'm finally satisfied with the face and background. Then the added enigmas of hands and fingers begin.

Marie continued to be passionate about music, and in 1943 she bought a secondhand Steinway for the Brown County studio. When two conductors of the Indianapolis Symphony Orchestra traveled to

Marie's cottage for a sitting, a city reporter came along and expressed surprise at the decor. The reporter wrote:

> The studio is an almost bleak little room with a nondescript jumble of furniture. There is a grand piano with an Indian print over it, a couple of uncomfortable looking straight chairs with faded red velvet cushions, and numerous glass jars filled with paint brushes. A half-empty bottle of maple sirup [sic] leans in one window. It was the portraits in the room that made it come to life.

Marie Goth became the first woman commissioned by a governor to paint his official portrait. Her painting of Indiana Governor Henry Frederick Schricker, created in 1952, depicts Schricker sitting:

> erect in a Windsor chair, a favorite of Goth's in her Brown County studio where the sittings were held. She has portrayed Governor Schricker in a cordial mood, his eyes fixed on the observer with an interested, sympathetic look. A twinkle in his eye and the upward curve of his mouth suggest his droll humor. The governor's trim gray suit is seen against a deep maroon curtain, and his necktie repeats the color of the background. Goth's style is bold, combining skillful brushwork with a good knowledge of color and design.

She also painted the portraits of other famous figures, including Will Hayes, a movie mogul who was so busy that he spent only a few moments at a time for his "sittings." Marie didn't mind, however, enjoying waiting in a spacious, luxurious apartment at the Waldorf, looking out over the skyline of New York City so familiar to her from her years in art school.

As Marie aged, the residents of Brown County looked after her, particularly as she mourned the loss of her sister Genevieve, who died in 1961. V. J. Cariani passed away eight years later. Marie continued to paint and stayed in touch through many letters with friends and relatives.

When Marie was eighty-seven, two of her paintings were accepted in the juried Hoosier Salon. However, she didn't live to attend the exhibition. In an obituary by Bruce Smith printed in the *Indianapolis Star* on January 23, 1975, it was reported that:

> an autopsy shows that Brown County artist Marie Goth, 87, had been bitten by a poisonous brown recluse spider before she died. This species of spider has been migrating into Indiana in recent years from the South. However, her death on [January] 9 resulted from head injuries suffered in a fall down a stairway. It is believed she became ill and disoriented from the spider's bite and this caused her to fall.

In a tribute published in the Brown County *Democrat* six months later, writer Abe Eye described Marie's legacy this way:

> Lyrically aesthetic, that's what Marie Goth is all about. Music's been most important to her virtually from birth in 1887. . . . Miss Goth's star, however, has risen dramatically in another sphere, placing her high in the select group of esteemed Indiana artists. Her eloquent portraits of leading figures and other personalities, hanging throughout the country, have brought distinction to our state and prideful community, earning numerous honors along the way. . . . Many wonder what went into the "making of Marie Goth"—the formula for "so called success," as she refers to her work, requires unrequited interest, some talent, dogged hard work and enjoying every motivated minute of it. "I don't need to take a vacation," she says, "painting is both my work and my diversion."

Marie wished to have her artistic legacy remembered and honored. Upon her death, Marie's estate was bequeathed, with conditions, to the Brown County Artist Guild. With the gift, Marie asked that the guild create a room dedicated to the memory of her and her longtime companion, V. J. Cariani, as well as to her sister and brother-in-law, Genevieve and Carl Graf. This room was to be kept up for a minimum of twenty years. If the guild no longer existed after that time or could not maintain the memorial, then the estate would revert to the Brown County Art Gallery—a rival organization. In asking for the agreement, Marie united the two groups in the honoring of Indiana's portrait artists.

BIBLIOGRAPHY

Frances Slocum

Bailey, G. S. "The Story of Frances Slocum." *The Morning Republic.* June 19,1869. Retrieved May 2005 from www.rootsweb.com/~inmiami/fslocum.html.

Dye, Kitty. *Maconaquah's Story: The Saga of Frances Slocum.* Port Clinton, Ohio: LeClere Publishing Company, 2000.

Gilman, Julia. *William Wells and Maconaquah, White Rose of the Miamis.* Cincinnati, Ohio: Jewel Publishing, 1985.

Meginness, John F. *Biography of Frances Slocum, The Lost Sister of Wyoming.* Williamsport, Penn.: Heller Brothers Printing House, 1891. Retrieved June 2006 from http://www.gbl.indiana.edu/archives/miamis21/M78_1a.html.

"Old Bible Owned by Scranton Woman Tells of Capture of [Frances Slocum] Lost Daughter of Wyoming." *Scranton (Penn.) Times,* October 3, 1916. Retrieved August 2005 from www.rootsweb.com/~scwhite/slocum/frances.html.

Peckham, H. H. *Captured by Indians: True Tales of Pioneer Survivors.* New Brunswick, N.J.: Rutgers University Press, 1954.

Phelps, Martha Bennett. *Frances Slocum: The Lost Sister of Wyoming.* 2nd ed. New York: The Knickerbocker Press, 1916.

Winger, Otho. *The Lost Sister among the Miamis.* Elgin, Ill.: The Elgin Press, 1936.

Rhoda M. Coffin

Johnson, Mary Coffin, ed. *Rhoda M. Coffin: Her Reminiscences, Addresses, Papers, and Ancestry.* New York: Grafton, 1910.

Johnson, Mary Coffin, and P. B. Coffin. *Charles F. Coffin: A Quaker Pioneer.* Richmond, Va.: Nicholson Printing Company, 1923.

Spencer, C. "Evangelism, Feminism and Social Reform: The Quaker Woman Minister and the Holiness Revival." *Quaker History* 1, vol. 80 (1999). Retrieved January 2006 from http://messiah .edu/whwe/articles/article6.htm

Swain, Ellen D. "From Benevolence to Reform: The Expanding Career of Mrs. Rhoda Coffin." *Indiana Magazine of History* 47 (September 2001): 190–217.

Mary Wright Sewall

Boomhower, Ray E. *But I Do Clamor: May Wright Sewall, A Life 1844–1920.* Zionsville: Guild Press of Indiana, 2001.

Hale, Hester Anne. *May Wright Sewall, Avowed Feminist.* Indiana Historical Society, Manuscripts and Archives Department, 1992. Manuscript Collection #BV 2638.

Minutes of National Woman Suffrage Association for the State of Indiana. Indiana Historical Society Records, 1887–1893. Manuscript Collection #BV 2612.

Sewall, May Wright. *Neither Dead nor Sleeping.* Indianapolis: The Bobbs-Merrill Company Publishers, 1920.

"The Suffrage Seekers: Indiana Women Who Want the Power of the Ballot Review Their Work, and Find That They Have Made Very Gratifying Progress—Addresses by Mrs. Gougar, Mrs. Sewall and Miss Anthony." *Indianapolis Journal,* May 3, 1887.

Virginia Claypool Meredith

Bartholomew, H. S. K. "Virginia C. Meredith." *Indiana Magazine of History* 35 (March 1939): 49–57.

"Meredith and Matthews." Purdue Legends website. Retrieved December 2005 from www2.itap.purdue.edu/periodicals/M.M.leg.html.

"Virginia Claypool Meredith (1848–1936)." Retrieved December 2005 from www.mrlinfo.org/history/biography/meredithvc.htm.

Eliza Ann Cooper Blaker

Harvey-Koelpin, Sally. *Blaker, Eliza Ann.* Learning to Give website. Retrieved November 2005 from www.learningtogive.org/papers/index.asp?bpid=78.

Indianapolis Free Kindergarten. "Minutes of the Executive Board and the Superintendent's Reports, 1884-1949." Indianapolis-Free Kindergarten Collection, Indianapolis Free Kindergarten Organizational Records, 1884-1914, 1917-1931, Manuscripts and Archives Department, Indiana Historical Society, Indianapolis, Indiana.

Roberts, Dawn. *Eliza Blaker's Life and Work.* Eliza Blaker Collection, Rare Books and Special Collections, The Irwin Library, Butler University, Indianapolis, Indiana, 1982.

Thornbrough, E. L. *Eliza A. Blaker: Her Life and Work.* Indianapolis: The Eliza A. Blaker Club and the Indiana Historical Society, 1956.

Juliet V. Humphreys Strauss

Boomhower, Ray E. *The Country Contributor: The Life and Times of Juliet V. Strauss* Caramel: Guild Press of Indiana, 1998.

"Indiana's Popular History: Juliet Strauss." Indiana Historical Society website. Retrieved September 2005 from http://www.indiana history.org/pop_hist/people/strauss.html.

Pearson, D. Forum. *Indianapolis Star Magazine,* August 31, 1980.

Gene Stratton Porter

Bailey, F. E. *Pioneer Days in the Wabash Valley: The Life of Gene Stratton Porter.* Logansport, Ind.: Hendricks Bros. Co. Printers, 1933.

"Gene Stratton Porter." *Indiana Historian,* September 1996, 1–15.

Gene Stratton Porter, Author and Naturalist. Indiana Department of Natural Resources, Indiana Division of Museums and Memorials, November 1974.

Long, Judith Reick. *Gene Stratton-Porter: Novelist and Naturalist.* Indianapolis: Indiana Historical Society, 1990.

Meehan, Jeannette Porter. *The Lady of the Limberlost: The Life and Letters of Gene Stratton-Porter.* Garden City, N.Y.: Doubleday, Doran & Company, Inc., 1928.

Morrow, Barbara Olenyik. *From Ben-Hur to Sister Carrie: Remembering the Lives and Works of Five Indiana Authors.* Indianapolis: Guild Press of Indiana, 1995.

Richards, B. F. *Gene Stratton Porter.* Boston: Twayne Publishers, 1980.

Saxton, Eugene F. *Gene Stratton-Porter: A Little Story of the Life and Work and Ideals of "The Bird Woman"* Garden City, N.Y.: Doubleday, Page and Company, 1926.

Shumaker, Arthur. *A History of Indiana Literature.* Indiana Historical Collections XLII, Indiana Historical Bureau, 1962.

Albion Fellows Bacon

Bacon, Albion Fellows. *Beauty for Ashes.* New York: Dodd, Mead, & Co. 1914.

———. *The Path to God.* New York and London: Harper & Brothers,1928.

Barrows, Robert G. *Albion Fellows Bacon: Indiana's Municipal Housekeeper.* Bloomington and Indianapolis: Indiana University Press, 2000.

Bennett, Helen Christine. "Albion Fellows Bacon." In *American Women in Civic Work,* 117-37. New York: Dodd, Mead & Co. 1915.

Boewe, Mary. "Annie & Albion: Reformers of Riverville." *Traces of Indiana and Midwestern History* 7, no. 1 (Winter 1995).

Madam C. J. Walker

Bundles, A'Lelia. *On Her Own Ground: The Life and Times of Madame C. J. Walker,* New York: Scribner, 2001.

"Focus—Madam C. J. Walker," *The Indiana Junior Historian.* Indiana Historical Bureau, State of Indiana, 1992.

"Madam C. J. Walker, 1867–1919 Entrepreneur, Philanthropist, Social Activist." Retrieved September 2005 from www.madamecjwalker.com.

Rooks, Noliwe Makada. *Hair-Raising: African American Women, Beauty Culture, and Madame C. J. Walker.* PhD diss., University of Iowa, 1994.

Wells, I. J. K, ed. "From Cabin to Castle: The Life Story of Madam C. J. Walker." *Color,* 2, no. 14 (December 1946) 4-12.

Marie Goth

"Indiana Governor Portrait Artist: Marie Goth (1887–1975), Indiana Governors' Portrait Collection, Indiana Historical Bureau." Retrieved December 2005 from http://www.statelib.lib.in.us/www/ihb/govportraits/goth.html.

Judd, Barbara, and Joanne M. Nesbit, ed. *Marie Goth: Painter of Portraits.* Nashville, Ind.: Nana's Books, 1996.

Morton, Thomas J. Papers, 1951–1975, bulk 1972–1975. Manuscript Collection, Indiana Historical Library, Indianapolis, SC3675.

Newton, J. V., and C. A. Weiss. *Skirting the Issue: Stories of Indiana's Historical Women Artists.* Indianapolis: Indiana Historical Society Press, 2004.

ABOUT THE AUTHORS

Anita K. Stalter and Rachel J. Lapp are a mother–daughter research and writing team from Goshen, Indiana.

Anita, a lifelong educator, has served as academic dean and vice president for academic affairs at Goshen College since 2001. Formerly a professor of education and chair of the education department at Goshen College, she holds a doctorate in curriculum, teaching, and educational policy from Michigan State University. In addition to academic and administrative leadership, she has published and given numerous professional presentations in areas of teacher education, multicultural classrooms, teachers as researchers, faith development in children and adolescents, and academic assessment.

Rachel, a former newspaper journalist, led publications, media relations, multimedia and other campus communication efforts as director of public relations at Goshen College for eight years. She served as faculty advisor to the college's student newspaper for a year, and recently joined an academic colleague in two initiatives of the Communication Departments Peace and Justice Journalism Project, co-leading small groups of students who traveled to El Salvador to learn about the international coffee market and fair trade coffee, and to Swaziland to report about the HIV/AIDS pandemic. Rachel is pursuing a master's degree in multicultural communication at DePaul University in Chicago and works as an editor. She is actively engaged in the promotion of cultural arts at community, national, and international levels.